BUCKET
~ TO ~
GREECE

Volume 10

V.D. BUCKET

Editor: James Scraper

Proofreader: Alan Wood

Cover: German Creative

Interior Format: The Book Khaleesi

Other Books in the
Bucket to Greece Series

Chapter 1

A Sorry Excuse for a Man Cave

W hat have we been reduced to, Victor?" Barry lamented. "Lounging about on a couple of damp cushions that have lost all their stuffing…"

"In a frog infested wooden shed, to boot," I added with a grimace befitting our grimy bolthole. A dank fusty smell pervaded the place, though it was hard to pinpoint if it came from the bags of goat droppings that Cynthia spread liberally in the vegetable garden or something more sinister. Barry's garden shed was certainly a sorry excuse for a man cave.

"It's all a bit of a comedown from the days

when we used to take refuge from life's tribulations in your superior downstairs storage," Barry observed.

"Violet Burke confiscated my key to the *apothiki* after that incident when *Kapetainos* Vasos burst in on me in the bath," I sighed. "It's a bit of a cheek considering it is technically my property and my mother is only the tenant."

"Even tenants have the right to come home without discovering their landlords wallowing in the bathtub," Barry argued.

"Not freeloading ones. Oh, for goodness sake," I complained, shaking my leg to dislodge a stubborn frog. "You ought to try vinegar, Barry."

"I swear by the stuff…"

"As a frog deterrent," I clarified.

"Why are you hiding out in here, anyway?" Barry asked, grabbing the frog and setting it loose through a hole in the wooden planks.

"I'm avoiding Norman. He's more difficult to shake off than a nasty dose of fleas on a feral cat ferreting for food in the bins."

Ever since Norman had managed to concoct a passable imitation of the Greek version of beef with olives, *vodino katsaroles me elies*, that I had demonstrated in my first cookery class, he had convinced himself he was the next Galloping Gourmet. Doreen reported that my cookery classes had infused Norman with a new get-up-and-go. Whilst I am all in favour of a bit of enthusiasm, I was not particularly enthused about Norman's sudden propensity for getting-up-and-going to my kitchen whenever the fancy took him, to pick my brain on techniques for perfecting choux pastry or adding a decorative glaze. Although puddings are not really my forte, Norman insists on considering me the oracle on anything with even a passing acquaintance with an oven.

Norman's newly discovered interest in cooking had developed into a passion for experimenting with elaborate patisserie desserts, although he hasn't quite got the hang of them yet. Doreen is forever coming up with ingenious places to hide his blow torch, convinced he will end up singeing the cat instead of caramelising the crème brulee. Still, at least Norman's new confectionery hobby keeps him away from the bottle.

"What about you?" I asked. "Why are you skulking away in here?"

Hanging his head, Barry confessed, "I'm in the doghouse again."

His general bearing definitely resembled that of a cowed canine.

"I suppose Cynthia is still sulking about that vile cat of hers being on the missing list," I guessed.

My sister-in-law had been distinctly off with

me lately since it came out that Violet Burke had hurled Kouneli into the back of a passing pickup that sped off to who only knows where. Despite my protestations that my mother's antics were nothing to do with me, apparently I was guilty by association. Even if Violet Burke had bucketed up the cat and abandoned it at the nearest railway station, there would still be no logic in Cynthia blaming me.

"No, Cyn has convinced herself that the cat is intelligent enough to find its way home...eventually." The way Barry rolled his eyes as he spoke indicated he considered the idea preposterous. "I'm being put through the wringer now because Cynthia's mother has been on the blower trying to guilt her into spending Christmas with them in England."

"That Trout woman has a nerve after the way she carried on over here, making out that you weren't good enough for her daughter," I said, bristling with righteous indignation on behalf of my brother-in-law. "Surely you aren't even entertaining the notion."

"Of course I'm not. I put my foot down and told Cynthia straight that I'm not spending my time with that poisonous pair. She only went and got the hump when I suggested she could always go and visit them without me."

"Well, that strikes me as an eminently reasonable compromise," I said.

"Cynthia expected me to rise up as her champion defender and tell the Trouts where to get off…"

"But if you'd done that then you'd probably be in the doghouse for insulting her mother. It sounds to me as though you just can't win, Barry," I sympathised.

"Which is why I am lying low in the shed until Cynthia sees sense." The look of resignation on Barry's face accentuated his point.

"It's typical of that Trout woman to start banging on about Christmas when we're barely into December," I pointed out. "I do loathe the way the Nativity festival has become so commercialised. At least over here, the Greeks have the right idea. They hardly make a fuss at all: you don't see the locals putting up vulgar displays of Christmas lights."

"That's probably because any attempt to put on a show would cause a mass power blackout. Anyway, electricity isn't cheap you know," Barry said pragmatically.

"The price of electricity hasn't deterred Norman from his plan to decorate the front of his house with traffic cones illuminated with fairy lights," I sighed.

"How is Marigold?" Barry changed the subject. I can't say I blame him: there is absolutely nothing riveting about traffic cones, even if they are bedecked in flashing lights. Norman's festive decorating plans would likely result in a load of rubbernecking, with any passing drivers slowing down to gawp at what they imagine to be a grisly traffic accident.

"Your sister is not in the best of moods. I told her that we'll have to tighten our belts in the coming months. That luxury break in Athens was a drain on my finances," I confided. Marigold had embraced the concept of luxury with a tad too much relish for my liking when I collected her at the airport after her jaunt to England. "I barely turn a profit from my cookery classes by the time I've splashed out on name badges and chalk..."

"No sign of any other work to tide you over for the winter?"

"Nothing that appeals..."

"That white collar work of yours back in England didn't really train you for getting your hands dirty with manual labour or olive picking..."

"Believe me, my hands went in some thoroughly disgusting places," I shuddered.

"It's not as though you have to work," Barry pointed out.

"I'm not quite ready for the scrapheap yet. You know how I like to keep busy," I reminded him.

"Have you considered expanding your classes?

They may be more lucrative if you signed up more pupils," Barry suggested.

"It's certainly an idea. Sherry tells me that word of my cookery classes has spread amongst the expats further afield from Meli and has sparked quite a bit of interest," I said.

"There's diddly-squat else for most of them to do out of season. It's hardly the weather for sunbathing and most of the bars are closed."

Acknowledging Barry's point with a nod, I patted myself on the back for my decision to move to a small mountain village where we had made it our mission to integrate with the locals. In some of the more touristy areas it struck me that the expat contingent treated their lives in Greece as akin to a permanent holiday, a veritable social whirl of Brits getting together. In contrast, most of the members of the extended Bucket family kept their noses to the grindstone, eking out a living with seasonal work and out of season pickings. Marigold encouraged me to continue earning a crust, saying she wasn't quite ready to adapt to having me underfoot on a permanent basis.

"I'm not keen on the idea of inviting a bunch of random Brits that I don't know into my kitchen," I said.

"You could sell yourself as a roving cookery instructor and make house calls down on the coast.

After all, teaching is a portable skill," Barry suggested.

"That's not a bad idea at all, Barry," I said. Taking my culinary instruction out on the road had potential if the people choosing to host my classes could ensure their kitchens were germ free zones.

"Me and Vangelis have some work starting next week in one of the popular tourist villages. A couple from Yorkshire want us to lay some crazy paving paths in their garden and build miniature walls round their olive trees. I'll spread the word about your classes if you like."

"I suppose if they can afford to shell out on superfluous walls, they can afford to splurge on my classes," I agreed.

"I expect that Marigold is planning to bleed you dry with that poncy vow renewal service she's fixated on. She's never shut up about it since she got home from Manchester," Barry laughed.

"It's no laughing matter," I groaned.

"Well it was your idea," Barry reminded me. "Surely you realised what you were letting yourself in for."

"For the umpteenth time, Barry, I simply blurted it out to convince Sherry that rather than being an available object of fancy, I was fully committed to my marriage." My words were met with a smirk. Exasperated, I continued, "I was hardly to know that Marigold would interpret my foot-in-mouth moment as a grand romantic gesture. Now she's blathering on about doing it barefoot on the beach. I ask you, can you picture me barefoot in a suit?"

"Well, I would have said never until you sprouted that fluff on your chin…"

"It's a goatee," I corrected.

"In your dreams, Victor," Barry snorted. "If it wasn't for your short back and sides, you'd look like a hippie. You might have been able to carry it off if you hadn't gone and shaved off the matching tache, but on its own that sorry excuse for a beard just looks like wispy bumfluff."

"I had no choice but to shave off the tache. I ended up singeing my nostril hair when I applied the Grecian 2000 to my moustache. Goodness knows how long it had been lurking in the back of Harold's bathroom cabinet." Although I spoke with as much dignity as I could muster, it had been the height of humiliation conducting my latest cookery class with balled up wads of cotton wool protruding from my nostrils.

"Blimey, Victor, that sounds painful. I might not have succumbed to the grey yet, but even I know that you can't go round randomly applying out-of-date chemicals to the hair on different bits of your body…"

"Not succumbed indeed," I chortled. "Do you think I don't know that you get Marigold to tweeze your grey hairs out?"

"Not so loud, Victor. I don't want Cynthia hearing…"

"After seeing that photo of you with the mullet, I hardly think a few grey hairs are going to faze your wife."

Ignoring my comment, Barry retorted, "You should have just boot polished the tache. Vangelis swears it works on his chest hairs."

"Until he gets caught in the rain," I laughed, recalling the smudged mess bleeding through Vangelis' shirt when he was soaked in a recent downpour.

The shed door creaked on its hinges. I exchanged a worried look with Barry. We braced ourselves, anticipating that Norman or Cynthia had discovered our hideout. It was quite a relief when my wife walked in.

"There you are, Victor. I've been looking for you everywhere," Marigold tutted. "What on earth are you both doing skulking in here?"

"I just popped by to give Barry a bit of advice on ridding the shed of frogs," I improvised.

"I'm sure you gained a wealth of knowledge ridding grubby takeaways of intrusive amphibians," Marigold shot back sarcastically.

"Well there was that pretentious French place

next to the boating pond," I muttered under my breath. In truth, the frog that I had spied hopping around in the kitchen had been part of the chef's fresh ingredients rather than an indication of an infestation of the local pond life. As I recall, I had let Julien off with a stern warning to keep his ingredients under better control. I often found it prudent to take a practical approach during my illustrious career as a public health inspector.

"More to the point, what are you doing in my shed?" Barry asked Marigold, his tone unusually unwelcoming. I suppose his attitude was justified: no red-blooded man cares to have his man cave invaded by the fairer sex.

"Cynthia said that she saw the two of you sneaking in here. Victor, we're going out to dinner this evening…"

"It's the first I've heard of it," I grumbled. I had been looking forward to a quiet evening at home, curled up in front of a blazing log fire with my newly acquired copy of 'Hygiene for Management'. It was the latest addition and I do like to keep abreast of any new developments in environmental health procedures: one never knows when such knowledge will come in handy.

"Yes, well, it's a rather impromptu gathering of the expat dining club. Doreen is hosting. She said that Norman has been experimenting so much in the kitchen that she may as well throw a dinner party rather than seeing good food go to waste. If nothing else, it's an excuse for a good knees-up," Marigold said with forced jollity.

I inwardly cringed: after two straight years of being dragged along to the expat dining club, I have yet to describe one of the soirees as a good knees-up. Recalling that prior to my first cookery class, Norman had found the complexity of making a sandwich a culinary challenge too far, I protested, "He's only been cooking for three weeks. I doubt that he's managed to produce anything edible yet."

"But it has been an intensive three weeks. Doreen says that Norman is so keen that he's completely taken over the kitchen; she can't even get a look in," Marigold revealed. "He's been bashing around in there from dawn to dusk."

"Well, if it's all the same to you, I'd rather not be one of his guinea pigs," I said.

"Don't be ridiculous, darling. You can't expect me to go without you. It would only fuel those nasty rumours that I've left you," Marigold cajoled.

"Tell me Doreen hasn't roped me and Cyn in too," Barry groaned.

"No, Cynthia got out of it by saying she didn't want to take Anastasia out in the cold…"

"Thank goodness for that," Barry sighed in relief.

"So you'll be coming along with me and Victor," Marigold said, her voice brokering no argument.

"You can't expect me to be the odd man out at a dinner party," Barry cleverly wheedled. "Doreen won't like having odd numbers."

"You won't be odd, Barry, you'll be escorting Victor's mother," Marigold announced. "Now, why you had to go upsetting Cynthia by bringing up her ghastly parents?"

Lowering his head, Barry bit his tongue. It was pointless arguing if Cynthia and Marigold had joined forces.

"Chop chop, Victor," Marigold hurried me. "You need to shave that fluff off your chin before we go to Doreen's place. I tolerated you looking like a down-and-out when you insisted it was a vital piece of olive picking equipment for when you helped out Dimitris…"

Barry raised his eyebrows questioningly.

"To keep my chin warm in the chill of the early morning," I explained.

"But it will have to go now," Marigold insisted. "I'm not having you showing me up by turning up at an expat dinner party looking like an escaped convict on the run."

"Leave it out, Sis. How many times are you going to rake up that sorry business about Victor being arrested?"

Barry's protest on my behalf barely registered, my mind flooded with discomfiting memories of my recent arrest and unjust incarceration.

Chapter 2

Fluent in Effluent

Although I had been in two minds over whether to come clean about my arrest to Marigold on her return from Manchester, it had struck me that fessing up was undoubtedly the best policy. Much as I would have preferred to skirt the truth, it seemed inevitable that the whole sorry business would come out if I resorted to a spot of subterfuge and attempted to keep it from my wife. Keeping things under wrap in Meli is nigh on impossible since gossip is the lifeblood of the village: I envisaged a marital disaster if Marigold happened to discover from some random blabbermouth that I now boast a criminal record.

On the Sunday morning following *Kapetainos* Vasos blundering in on my taking a bath in the *apothiki*, I was due to manage the shop for the day. Tina, the shopkeeper, was finally due to get rid of her wart-faced hag of a mother, Despina, who had been recuperating in the apartment above the shop following an operation for a new knee. Tina, having been at the beck and call of the querulous demands of the malicious old trout, was by then quite desperate to drive Despina back to her own home. It was scheduled to be my last day working in the shop: whilst I had been happy to step into the breach and help out by serving the local community, my stint behind the counter had revealed that shop keeping is not my natural forte.

As the piercing scream of the alarm clock penetrated my stupor on that Sunday morning, it dawned on me that I was suffering from the repercussions of the night before. Once *Kapetainos* Vasos had recovered from his bout of convulsive laughter, he had insisted on dragging me out for a night of debauched carousing and picking up women, a night I preferred not to dwell on in my delicate condition. The fetid stench of fishy breath wafting over from the adjacent pillow filled me with horror as I desperately tried to recall how the night before had ended up: Marigold would never forgive me if I had let the good Captain pour so much *ouzo* down my throat that I had allowed myself to be taken advantage of by some random predatory woman. Opening one eye warily, I sighed in relief to see nothing more disturbing than Clawsome stretched out next to me, hogging Marigold's pillow. The persistent crow of the rooster in the hen house pecked away like a jackhammer in my skull, nothing short of torture in my hungover state. Despite my pounding head, I made a concerted effort to crawl out of bed. I had no intention of letting Tina down at the last minute: it seems I have inherited Violet Burke's habit of never throwing a sickie.

Groping my way to the bathroom, I forced down a couple of *Depon*: to say that the image staring back at me from the bathroom mirror was not a pleasant sight is an understatement. Grey faced and haggard, my straggly growth of beard only served to accentuate my dissolute appearance. Barely recognising the scruff in the mirror, I realised the beard would have to go unless I wanted to scare away all of Tina's customers. Alas, my efforts to manipulate a cut-throat razor with shaking hands proved a challenge too far, though the resultant wads of toilet paper stuck to my bleeding cuts did disguise some of my facial growth, even if they did nothing to enhance my appearance.

After downing a gallon of strong black coffee, I

made my way to the shop, shielding my eyes from the dazzling early morning sunshine behind a pair of dark glasses. The strong wind whipping against my face proved that the beard I was cultivating as a chin warmer was ineffective against the cold morning air, though it did dislodge my makeshift plasters, leaving a strew of blood smeared toilet paper in my wake. A carrier bag picked up by the wind flew directly towards my head. Ducking to avoid being slapped in the face by cold plastic, I was instead slapped in the cheek by a bunch of olives hanging forlornly from the drooping branch of an olive tree. Barely avoiding tripping over the swirl of fur that shot between my legs, I thought for one moment that Cynthia's vile cat had returned to the village. Shaking my head, I realised my hungover brain must be playing tricks on me and that Pickles bore more of a resemblance to its mutant father than I had previously registered.

Despite the early hour, Tina was already busy piling bags and cases into her car outside the shop, evidence that she wasn't wasting a moment in getting shot of her wart-faced old bat of a mother at the first opportunity.

"Victor, you are the lifesaver," Tina trilled, oblivious to my unkempt appearance.

"I see that you're making an early start," I commented.

"The sooner I to get the *mama* settle in her own house, the better. It will be much the work to make everything the clean for her but I hope to be back before you to close the shop."

My heart sank at Tina's words. Since the shop remained open until 5pm on Sundays, a long day stretched in front of me.

"*Ela, Mama, grigora,*" Tina called into the wind, telling her mother to hurry. I bristled at the sight of Despina hobbling slowly towards the car, a vine-garish expression on her face. Her exaggerated show of leaning heavily on a walking stick was no doubt for Tina's benefit, a deliberate ploy to rub Tina's nose in her guilt about sending her mother home. I had managed to avoid the poisonous crone since she had spread the baseless rumours that Marigold had left me, knowing no good would come from confronting her. With Despina now in such close range, it took a concerted effort to keep my distance and hold my tongue.

"*Min me viazeis, den boro na perpatiso,*" Despina snapped, telling her daughter not to rush her, she could hardly walk.

"*O giatros eipe oti den chreiazeste to ravdi,*" Tina said, telling her mother that the doctor had said she didn't need a stick.

"She drag it out for, how you say, the plebiscite for the sympathy," a familiar voice hissed in my ear.

"The sympathy vote," I corrected as Spiros threw an arm around my shoulder.

"Tina to say the doctor to say the new knee to give the Despina the leg of the teenage," Spiros confided.

"Like you said, she's after the sympathy vote," I concurred. Despite my usually impeccable good manners, I made no effort to step forward to assist the old woman. Still bristling from the malevolent rumours Despina had started, I knew that if I got any closer, I might be tempted to wring her neck. As I abhor violence, I had decided that the best course of action was to avoid all contact with Despina and I determined to continue ignoring her now.

"You are looking the rough, Victor," Spiros observed.

"Remind me never to go out on the town with *Kapetainos* Vasos ever again," I grimaced.

The two of us remained rooted to the spot, watching Despina plod laboriously towards the vehicle. Drawing level with the passenger door, she fired a contemptuous look in my direction before turning to her daughter. Spewing her customary venom, Despina didn't bother to lower her voice. *"Den théleis na fýgeis apó to magazí me aftón ton ántra, ísos i gynaíka tou na min ton áfise, ísos na tis taïzei to komméno sóma sta kotopoula."*

Even though I could discern she was deliberately goading me, I was in no fit state to translate her words. Fortunately, Spiros was on hand to provide a running commentary. "The Despina say to the Tina, you not to want to leave the shop with that man. She say maybe the wife not to leave you, maybe you feed her chopped up body to the chickens."

Spiros was already physically restraining me when Tina snapped at her mother, "*Pos boreite na peite kati tetoio? Zitisete syngnomi ston Victor,*" meaning, 'How can you say such a thing? Apologise to Victor.'

"*Den tha. Koitaxte ton, tha borouse na taisei to soma tis gynaikas tou me choiro tou Dimitri,*" Despina shot back with a vindictive smirk.

"What?" I spluttered. Surely I must have misheard; even Despina could not publicly make such wild accusations.

"She say she not to apologise. She say to look at you, you could have feed your the wife's body to the Dimitris' pig," Spiros helpfully translated.

"Unhand me, Spiro. I refuse to have my reputation maligned by that evil witch," I cried, struggling against Spiros' by now firm grip on my torso as he helpfully translated my words for Despina.

A triumphant look appeared in Despina's eye; she had been willing me to rise to the bait. Staring directly at me, she fired back that I clearly had no respect for women: listen to the way I just called her an evil witch.

"I can think of worse things to call you than that," I yelled.

"Ti leei?" Despina shouted, demanding to know what I'd said as she didn't understand my English words and Spiros hadn't bothered to translate, belatedly catching on that his helpful sallies were simply throwing more fuel on the fire.

Seeing red, I was taken by surprise with the stream of Greek expletives spontaneously spouting from my mouth. I had no idea that I was so fluent in foul-mouthed Greek, uttering the sort of swear words that would never pass my lips in English and which I would never allow to soil these pages. Clearly the influence of my brother-in-law's mastery of builders' Greek had subconsciously rubbed off on me.

Feigning fear, Despina waved her walking stick around as though to fend me off, even though I was still rooted to the spot. Tina, clearly mortified by her mother's ridiculous accusations that I had done away with my wife, lost her temper. Shouting at her mother, Tina pointed out that Despina's lies were slanderous.

"Tina, koita, i Despina den chreiazetai katholou afto to ravdi," Spiros yelled before turning to me and

saying in English, "I tell to Tina to look, the Despina not to need the stick at all."

"She's a fraud," I agreed, noting Despina's unwavering balance as she waved the walking stick over her head in a threatening gesture. "It's a pity the hospital didn't kit her out with a new tongue instead of a new knee."

Bundling Despina into the car, Tina warned her to shut up, "*Isychia, Mitera*," before turning to me and shrugging apologetically. "Victor, I am so the sorry for the nasty mother."

"It's not your fault, Tina, but if you take my advice, you will keep your mother away from village," I said. "When Marigold returns from Manchester, she may not have my self-restraint when it comes to Despina's evil tongue."

"You have to the shock me, Victor," Spiros said, finally relinquishing his firm hold as Tina's car pulled away. "I never before to hear you use the Greek with so much the effluent."

"With so much effluence…" I began to correct my friend before hesitating. On consideration, the invective that I had unleashed upon Despina had indeed been a deluge of sewage. "I'd better open the shop."

"I come inside and make the strong coffee," Spiros offered. As I fumbled around with the key to the shop, the undertaker lightened the mood with a joke. "The Despina is the mad, the insane. Everyone to know you would never to feed the Marigold body to the chicken because it would to break all your the hygiene rule."

"I might make an exception for Despina's riddled old carcass," I said in all seriousness.

By the time we had downed a couple of coffees, I was beginning to feel almost human again. It was just as well because the shop would begin to fill up when Papas Andreas finished his regular Sunday service. As Spiros took his leave, I began to make an inventory of which canned foods were needed to fill the gaps on the shelves. It appeared that Tina had recently done a roaring trade in tinned octopus in garlic sauce, cans of butter beans in tomato sauce *gigantes*, and jars of Merenda hazelnut spread. Filling a basket with the requisite items in the stockroom, I heard the shop bell tinkle and girded myself to deal with the first of the customers.

"It's a relief to see you working today, Victor," Norman announced as I greeted him. "I've decided to tackle that beef and olive dish you showed us in class for Sunday dinner. I wrote down that phrase for asking to have the meat cut up, but I'm not sure I could get my tongue round it."

Norman's words reminded me that although Kyria Kompogiannopoulou was supposed to be working alongside me, she had yet to make an appearance. I was pretty certain that my hangover would trump her bladder on the excuses for being tardy scale.

"So, what can I get you, Norman?"

"Stewing beef. For that casserole you made. And could you cut it up please?"

"It would be good for your chopping skills to learn how to do it yourself," I advised. Even the thought of wrapping a slab of beef in waxed paper made my stomach churn, never mind cutting it into neat little cubes for Norman.

"How do you say the customer is always right, in Greek?" Norman retorted.

"I'm not here to give you free Greek lessons," I snapped in annoyance, pulling a white pinny over my head and scouring my hands before handling the meat. Thinking that by rights I should be delegating this unpleasant task to my minion, I made a concerted effort to overcome my reluctance to use telephone Greek and dialled Kyria Kompogiannopoulou's number. Considering how I had taken Despina down a peg or two in flawless Greek, I ought to be able to manage to reprimand my Greek assistant for being late. As my call went unanswered, I presumed she must be on her way and reluctantly set to cutting the meat.

"You're looking a bit rough round the edges,"

Norman commented. "I suppose that with Marigold away, you can let yourself go. No woman to nag you about shaving, eh."

"I am growing a beard," I snapped, cursing under my breath as I swung the cleaver at the meat and blood splattered all over my pristine white pinny.

"Now, do the olives have to be pip free or doesn't it matter?" Norman asked.

"The word is pitted, Norman, pitted," I schooled him.

"Pitted," he repeated, as though it was a foreign word he had yet to master.

Hoping he choked on the things, I added, "No need to buy pitted olives, the ones with the stones in will do nicely." Even if he didn't choke on them, he might break a tooth with any luck. An hour in the dentist's chair and a mouth numbing injection ought to shut him up. My fantasy of the sadistic dentist who had worked on Marigold's broken filling doing unspeakable things to Norman was interrupted by the arrival of Kyria Kompogiannopoulou.

"*Eisai argopromimeni*," I snapped. Dispensing with the usual greeting, I told her she was late.

"*Einai Kyriaki. Echo paei stin ekklissia*," she replied, telling me it was Sunday and she had been in church.

Before I had the chance to chastise her for not letting me know she intended to roll in late, she had dashed off to the toilet. I reflected that to a good Orthodox Christian woman, her religious duty trumped skivvying in the shop for a pittance.

"You're most welcome to join us for Sunday dinner," Norman invited as I rung up his purchases. "After all, I'd never be experimenting in the kitchen if it wasn't down to you."

"I'll pass, if you don't mind, Norman. I'll be slaving away in here until past sunset." I had no intention of taste testing Norman's first experimental foray into cooking, even if it was my own tried and tested recipe. Still, as I reflected that his offer was kindly meant, I hastily substituted his jar of olives for pitted ones. If I wasn't careful, I was in danger of turning as curdled as Despina.

The rest of the morning passed in a flurry of activity, restocking shelves and serving demanding customers. The latter were particularly trying, either pointing out how rough I was looking or sympathising with me because they had heard that Marigold had left me. I was soon almost hoarse from explaining that I was cultivating an olive picking beard and that my wife, who was holidaying in England, had every intention of returning to the bosom of her loving husband.

In a lull between customers, Kyria Kompogiannopoulou urged me to take a break and enjoy the coffee she had brewed. Patting my arm in a motherly way, she told me that Despina was a horrible gossip and anyone could see how much Marigold loved me.

"*Sas efcharisto, Kyria Kompogiannopoulou,*" I thanked her, touched by the genuine affection in her voice.

"*Nomizo oti irthe i ora na ma kaleseis Sofia.*" Saying she thought it was time that I started to call her Sofia, she winked at me.

I felt quite honoured, as though I had passed some kind of test. Sipping my coffee, I winked back at her, saying, "*Kyria Sofia.*" It was only fitting that I addressed her respectfully by using the Greek word for Mrs in front of her given name; after all, she was a grandmother.

Our moment of bonding was interrupted by the arrival of Papas Andreas. Addressing my co-worker, he told her that he had missed her in church that morning. Flushing to the roots of her hair, Sofia muttered something about her bladder before rushing off to take refuge in the toilet.

Chapter 3

A Shared Passion for Galaktoboureko

M ust you always exaggerate, Barry? Victor does not have a criminal record," Marigold protested, narrowly avoiding squashing a rather anaemic looking frog as she petulantly stamped her foot to emphasise the point.

"You're splitting hairs. You know full well that he went and got himself arrested." Even though Barry had just accused Marigold of raking up my arrest, her denial seemingly goaded Barry into rubbing my nose in it.

Their petty bickering snapped me out of my reverie and back to the reality of the dank frog-infested shed: at least the shed was an improvement on the cell in the police station where I had ended up on that fateful Sunday. As Marigold and Barry squabbled about my brush with the law, my thoughts drifted back to the mortifying moment when the police had arrived at the shop and dragged me away.

Despite living in Greece for two years, that was the first time I had encountered any of the local constabulary in Meli itself. Since the only crime in the village comprised Cynthia's vile cat raping its way through the neighbourhood feral population and Kostis discharging the odd pot-shot outside the permitted hunting season, there really was no need for a local Bobby on the beat. The nearest police station, or *Astynomiko Tmima* as it is known in Greek, was a good forty minutes' drive away. The only time I had darkened its doors was on the occasion when I had accompanied Spiros there to apply for my resident's permit: at that time I had been more than happy to leave all the talking to my friend, preferring not to draw any undue attention to myself.

Sipping my coffee, my eyes were drawn to a police car parking up outside. Two uniformed officers emerged: I couldn't help but notice how smart they looked in their official regalia. After briefly conferring, one entered the shop whilst the other remained outside, lounging against the cop car smoking a cigarette. My natural assumption was that the young policeman was a customer, perchance stopping by to purchase a couple of takeaway coffees. However, his stern expression soon disabused me of the notion.

Firing a steely glare in my direction, the young officer looked me up and down, taking in my generally dissolute appearance and staring just a tad too long at my blood stained apron, disdain stamped on his face. Despite being a law-abiding citizen with nothing to fear from the police presence, I found myself fidgeting nervously under his relentless gaze. It was only when I recalled the occasion when Tina's mother had been arrested for illegal Sunday trading that I began to wonder if I had unwittingly become embroiled in something unlawful. Although I hadn't personally witnessed Despina's arrest, Marigold had recounted the tale with glee, the flurry of police action brightening up an otherwise dull Sunday for the villagers.

Slapping a worried smile on my face, I waited in vain for the policeman to place an order for coffee or cigarettes.

"*Boro na do tin adeia gia synallages tin Kyriaki.*" Although the officer's tone was cordial, his stance was all business as he asked if he could see the permit for Sunday trading. Recalling Spiros' sage advice that if the police ever stopped me whilst I was driving, I should innocently recite 'I don't understand' until they became so bored they lost interest, I decided to apply his handy tip to the current situation.

"*Den katalavaino,*" I whimpered, shrugging my shoulders for emphasis.

"*Thelei na dei tin adeia gia synallages tin Kyriaki,*" Kyria Kompogiannopoulou piped up, telling me that he wanted to see the permit. Wishing that she was still locked in the toilet, I silently cursed her intervention, doubly cursing her when she helpfully jogged my memory by repeating the Greek word for permit, "*Victor, i adeia.*"

Unsure how I was going to be able to square my stated non-understanding of the Greek language with Kyria Kompogiannopoulou speaking directly to me in Greek, I moronically resorted to repeating, "*Den katalavaino.*"

The policeman belatedly caught on that I wasn't a native Greek: perchance my rather unkempt appearance confused him. Whilst I would usually be flattered to be mistaken for a born and bred local, this hardly seemed the appropriate occasion to celebrate. Switching to tentative English, the policeman barked, "You, permission."

Fumbling in my trouser pocket, I produced a crumpled copy of my latest electricity bill, handing it over with a trembling hand. Casting a disdainful glance over my proffered paper, the policeman stated, "No good."

Although I realised he was stating the obvious since my electricity bill bore no resemblance to any official permit related to Sunday trading, I considered it expedient to stall him, having no clue where Tina kept her paperwork. Recalling that my passport was in the inside pocket of my jacket hanging up in the stockroom, I held up a couple of fingers to indicate that I would be back in a jiffy. The policeman's frown made me worry that I had inadvertently made a rude gesture in Greek: there may be some dire penalty for disrespecting a representative of the law. He was certainly less than impressed when a minute later I produced my passport and residence permit.

"No good. Shop permit," the policeman reiterated, maintaining a tight grip on my passport as he took a long look at the photograph, no doubt comparing my clean shaven celluloid image to the blood stained scruff in front of him. Inwardly chastising myself for failing to maintain my usual impeccable standards of personal hygiene, my thoughts went into overdrive. It struck me that it would be the height of stupidity for Tina to have failed to sort out the necessary permit after the previous arrest for illegal Sunday trading. However, I was clueless if she had done so: for all I knew, she may have continued to brazenly flout the law.

"Well, it isn't actually my shop and I don't know where the paperwork would be. I'm just helping out a friend because her mother is ill," I stuttered, worried that I may end up being deported if I admitted to working for cash-in-hand without declaring my taxes.

"*Ti les?*" Kyria Kompogiannopoulou demanded to know what I was saying. Her question rather put me on the spot: I could hardly respond whilst maintaining the pretence that I didn't understand what was going on. I decided the best policy was to ignore her and concentrate on the young policeman's attempt to communicate with me in faltering English.

"Permission," he repeated.

"*Prepei na tilefonisoume sti Tina kai na rotisoume pou einai i adeia*," Kyria Sophia said. Although her suggestion that we should telephone Tina and ask her where the permit was kept made sense, I felt obliged to keep up the pretence that I couldn't understand a word of her Greek babble. Nevertheless, the policeman gave the nod to the suggestion when Kyria Sofia extracted her mobile phone from her pocket.

The shop telephone began to ring in the background and the policeman indicated with a gesture that I might answer it. Scuttling through to the stockroom again, I lifted the receiver, only to hear Kyria Sofia asking, "*Tina, pou einai i adeia gia synallages tin Kyriaki?*" Clearly she thought the phone had been answered by Tina and she was asking her where she kept the permit for Sunday trading.

"*Ego eimai, Victor,*" I hissed, identifying myself before telling her to play along with the pretence that I didn't understand Greek because I didn't know if Tina had a permit.

"*Victor? Den katalavaino ta Ellinika sou.*" Her response that she didn't understand my Greek proved once and for all that my attempts to communicate via the telephone in a foreign language were beyond pathetic. Still, her abrupt termination of the call indicated that she realised the only telephone number she had for Tina was the one at the shop.

"You must to close shop and come the station," the policeman declared when I re-joined my assistant.

"But why?" I dared to challenge.

"No permit," he replied, before rounding the pair of us up and steering us out to the police car. Shuffling impatiently whilst I locked the shop, the policeman turned a deaf ear to Kyria Kompogiannopoulou's outraged complaint that they couldn't take away a grandmother with an extremely weak bladder. It did not escape my notice that her pleas to be spared arrest did not extend to me.

"I say, old chap, what's happening here? If my eyes don't deceive me, I'd swear it looks as though the police are about to cart you away," a plummy voice piped up behind me.

"It's just a misunderstanding…" I began to explain to Milton.

Undaunted by the police presence, he interrupted to whine, "I couldn't just get a couple of tins of cat food before they take you away? Clean forgot to stock up on the dratted stuff."

"Never mind your cat food, Milton, this is serious. Try and get hold of Spiros for me. Tell him a miscarriage of justice is taking place and I need his help urgently," I pleaded. "Oh, and tell him to try and locate Tina and see if she has a permit for Sunday trading. She's at her mother's house but we don't know the telephone number."

"Ah, trading on the Sabbath. I shouldn't think that kind of thing is really on in an Orthodox country. I can see why it might land you in a spot of bother, old chap," Milton tutted, ignoring the irony of his own attempt to do a bit of Sunday shopping. "Rum deal, them arresting you. Still, at least they haven't clapped you in handcuffs, what."

"Will you try and get hold of Spiros, please?" I begged Milton as the policemen bundled me into the back of their car along with Kyria Sofia.

"Leave it with me, old chap. I'm on it already," Milton assured me. "I hope that Spiros has got a spare tin of cat food going begging. That nice foreign girl of his is sure to have one, very fond of cats she is. Most inconvenient, what, you shutting up shop."

As the police car pulled out of the village square, I was relieved to notice there was no one around apart from Milton to witness my humiliation, a fact I put down to the inclement weather and my arrest coinciding with the Greek lunch time. On the other hand, I would have preferred someone with a bit more Greek nous to be able to step in to save me. I wasn't convinced that Milton would follow through and round up Spiros to come to my rescue. Milton could be a bit flaky at times: it didn't take much to distract him. I imagined a shapely turn of Violet Burke's ankle as she sped by on her bicycle would be enough to eradicate all memory of my arrest and my need for urgent assistance from his brain.

We had barely left the village when, to the irritation of the two policemen, Kyria Kompogiannnopoulou demanded the lavatory. After assuring them her need was urgent and that she was incapable of keeping her legs crossed until we reached the police station, they reluctantly parked up outside the first taverna we passed. Whilst the young policeman escorted her inside to use the facilities, I became an object of speculation to a large Greek family enjoying an outdoor lunch beneath a wooden awning, no doubt imagining that I was some master criminal about to get my comeuppance.

I wished that I'd had the foresight to grab my jacket to conceal the blood splattered apron I was still wearing, though I must confess to flaunting it in the face of the nosy child that had the cheek to press his grubby face up against the car window. The extended family looked less than impressed when said child's mockery morphed into cries of terror. Hastily grabbing the cardigan that Sofia had left on the seat, I threw it over my head before any of them decided to take a photographic record that may haunt me for posterity. Whilst the woolly cardigan served its purpose in concealing my visage from gawping children, it exacerbated the cold sweat dripping from my forehead and collecting in my armpits.

Once Kyria Kompogiannopoulou was back in the car and we resumed our journey to the police station, she began carping at the two policemen. She appeared to be more concerned that her daughter and grandson were visiting later and she wouldn't be able to make a start on her grandson's favourite *galaktoboureko*, than she was by her actual arrest. The second policeman, who had been silent until now, appeared to sympathise with her plight, recalling how his own granny used to make him the most divine milk custard pudding when he was a boy. Although I could follow most of their conversation, I thought it prudent to keep quiet about my own personal preference for adding just a pinch of nutmeg to the *galaktoboureko* recipe: I didn't want to risk giving the game away that I understood a little more Greek than I had let on to the police officer.

Eventually I tuned out, mentally questioning just how I had managed to end up in this sticky predicament. It hardly took a genius to work out that I had likely been dobbed in by a malicious busybody harbouring a grudge. Although I had restrained myself from lamping Despina that morning, I surmised that she had likely exacted her revenge for my expletive laden diatribe by phoning the police and reporting that the shop was doing a brisk business in illegal Sunday trading. Not only would such an underhand move allow the old crone to put one over on me, it might also result in temporarily closing down Tina's business. With the shop padlocked, Tina would be free to be on hand to continue ministering to her malingering mother. After mulling the matter over in my mind, I concluded that the only explanation for the police turning up in Meli was that Despina had ratted me out.

When Kyria Kompogiannopoulou demanded another toilet stop, I joined in the groans of frustration emitted by the policemen. Belatedly it dawned on me that the repeated stops for a bathroom could work to my advantage: by delaying our arrival at the police station it would give Milton more time to round up Spiros to come to my rescue. I considered it a tad hypocritical that the policeman escorting Sofia to the petrol station toilet didn't bother to stop and harangue the garage owner about producing a Sunday trading permit. Perhaps the arrest of myself and my co-worker fulfilled his weekly quota of rounding up dangerous criminals.

I maintained my pretence of not understanding a word of Greek when Kyria Kompogiannopoulou emerged from the petrol station lavatory. Announcing that the toilet was filthy, she suggested that I let my mother know in case there was a job going cleaning at the petrol station. Whilst pretending that I hadn't got a clue what she'd said, I discounted her suggestion immediately: there was no way that Violet Burke would be able to pedal as far as the garage or negotiate the steep hairpin bends as her borrowed bicycle didn't have any gears.

By the time we finally parked up at the police station, the older officer was quite engrossed in Kyria Kompogiannopoulou's pitiful saga about how the hospital was giving her bladder the run around. Having bonded over their shared passion for custardy *galaktoboureko,* he appeared to be overcome with guilt that they had insisted she came along to the police station. Whilst he continued to sympathise with Sofia, the younger officer indicated that I should follow him inside.

Chapter 4

Rallying Round

Escorted into the police station, I noticed it was hardly a hive of activity. Apart from the middle-aged sergeant sitting behind a desk blatantly ignoring the prominent 'No Smoking' sign, the place was empty. Whilst relieved that I wouldn't be expected to rub shoulders with common criminals, I would have preferred a tad more activity since my entrance may not have immediately attracted the attention of the officer in charge.

"Ti echoume edo?" the smoking sergeant asked the officer: 'What have we here?'

"Douleve sto katastima choris adeia Kyriakis," the

young policeman replied, telling him that I had been working in a shop without a Sunday permit. Although I maintained the pretence of not under-standing Greek, I understood that somehow Kyria Sofia had avoided been dragged inside, seemingly managing to wriggle out of being included in the charges. Perhaps there was method in her deliber-ately dangling the bribe of custardy treats to avoid custody.

The uniformed officer gesticulated towards me, telling the sergeant that I didn't speak any Greek, "*Afto den milaei Ellinika.*"

The sergeant looked at me quizzically. He didn't appear unduly perturbed by the sight of the rather dissolute figure I must cut, my unshaven and sweaty person all neatly wrapped up in a blood soaked apron. Even though I looked anything but my best, I expect he had seen much worse in his line of work. In comparison to his junior officers, the ser-geant hardly typified professional smartness, his own jowls in need of a good shave and his shirt front blotchy with a still damp coffee stain. After giving me the once over, he asked if I spoke Ger-man, "*Milao Germanika?*"

"English," I replied.

Without being prompted, the young officer handed my papers to the sergeant, volunteering the information that they were my passport and residence permit. "*To diavatirio kai i adeia diamonis tou.*"

As the sergeant scrutinised the papers with painstaking slowness, my attention was drawn to the posters gracing the wall behind his head, a mishmash of mug shots of wanted and no doubt dangerous criminals. I did a double take, recognising the dark features of Besnik, the Albanian foreman that had smuggled weapons over the border in a truck full of rabbits, shamefully abandoning Guzim's young wife Luljeta in Greece with no legal papers. Turning to follow my fixed gaze, the sergeant said in English, "Albanian bad man. You know?"

I exhaled in relief. The sergeant's mastery of basic English would spare me from pathetically parroting the Greek for I don't understand.

"He looks familiar," I said hesitantly. Not wanting the sergeant to get the impression that I was in the habit of fraternising with foreign gangsters, I clarified my statement by saying, "I think he did some building work for some British people not too far from here."

Crossing my fingers behind my back, I hoped that my casual remark would put some distance between Besnik's rather loose connection with Meli and his rather more familiar connection with the Albanian living in the shed at the bottom of my garden.

BUCKET TO GREECE (VOL.10)

"Yes, he make the show of being work hard," the sergeant said flatly, his tone giving nothing away. I wondered if he was aware that Besnik had been in the habit of running a bribery scam, offering brown envelopes stuffed with cash to local officials in order to speed up the process of securing white papers for any compatriots he employed with dodgy immigration status.

"He no good Albanian," the sergeant reiterated. Gesticulating expansively with his cigarette, he pointed to the adjacent wanted poster, contempt heavy in his tone. "He no good Kosovar."

No doubt it was the photograph of Besnik that prompted me to remember a conversation that I'd had with the Albanian foreman over a year ago. I vividly recalled him telling me about a Kosovar named Frenk attacking Tarek, one of Besnik's best Albanian workers, with a *Rugovo* dance sword. Whilst the victim of the vicious attack had survived, he had been summarily deported from Greece once his wounds had been stitched up, his attacker meanwhile making his escape. It appeared from the wanted poster that Frenk was still on the loose.

Before the sergeant could start interrogating me about my interest in the pair of miscreants on his wall, the second policeman escorted Kyria Kompogiannopoulou inside. As she began to express her hope that the toilet was clean, she stopped mid-sentence, exclaiming, "*Foti. Pos eisai? Den se echo dei edo kai aiones*." Her remarks were addressed to the sergeant, asking him how he was and saying she hadn't seen him for ages. Turning to the two policemen, she announced that she used to change the sergeant's nappies when he was a baby. As the sergeant turned puce with embarrassment, his two underlings struggled to control their mirth. As Kyria Sofia reminisced about how Fotis' family used to live in Meli back when he was a boy, I hoped that the sergeant's ties to my adopted village might work in my favour if Spiros ever showed up.

The telephone on the sergeant's desk rang, interrupting my fellow villager's trip down memory lane. After briefly conferring with the caller, the sergeant barked an order in Greek at the young policeman. As the officer took hold of my arm, I said, "*Den katalavaino*." There was no attempt to deflect when I told him I didn't understand since I genuinely couldn't translate the order.

"You wait. Man come," the sergeant told me as the young officer led me down a poorly lit corridor. Being a law abiding citizen with no experience of police station holding cells, I had no way of knowing if the room I was directed to was an actual cell or simply a drab waiting room. The windowless room was cold and gloomy, worn brown linoleum floor tiles erupting in places to reveal a grey concrete floor. Paint bubbled and peeled off the wall, brown patches on the ceiling evidence of heavy smokers being confined to the room. Bizarrely, an image of a brick lined prison cell with wobbly bars sprang to mind. It took me a moment to realise I had conjured up a picture of the prison environment depicted in 'Prisoner Cell Block H', the dire Australian soap opera that Marigold was addicted to: although I could hardly use it as a reliable comparison with a Greek holding cell, I noted that the room I had been directed to was at least free of bars.

The policeman indicated I should take a seat on the hard wooden bench running the length of the room, before swiftly marching off. To my relief, the door was left ajar, though that salient fact did little to comfort me. Alone, in what could possibly be a cell, it was brought home to me that I was a foreigner completely out of my depth and clueless to my immediate fate. My elaborate charade of feigning complete ignorance of the Greek language may have done me no favours, possibly exacerbating my status as an alien. However, fessing up at this late stage may make me look duplicitous and there was no guarantee I would be able to understand much of what was going on in if they rattled their words off with any great speed.

As the minutes ticked by, it dawned on me that

I should have exercised my right to demand a phone call: then again, I had no idea if the odd bit of police jargon that I had gleaned from my days of watching 'Dixon of Dock Green' was actually applicable to the circumstances I found myself in.

I wished that I had paid more attention to the news when that bunch of anoraks had been detained in a Greek prison for illegal plane spotting at Kalamata airport. As best I could recall, they had been held in a Greek prison for more than a month. I fervently hoped that it wouldn't take Spiros that long to spring me from the police station.

With my eyes fixed on the open door, I wondered if I should risk making my way back down the corridor to ask the sergeant if I could make a phone call to Spiros. Worried that such unauthorised movement on my part might lead to my being frogmarched right back to this drab room, the door summarily slammed and locked in my face, I decided to hold fast. Thus far, the sergeant had treated me decently enough, though the offer of a coffee wouldn't have gone amiss. I wondered if Kyria Sofia had been taken to a separate room reserved for female arrestees, or if she was enjoying preferential treatment by virtue of being a Greek grandma. For all I knew, she could be on her way home by now, leaving me to rot: she may have pulled a few nepotistic strings due to her familiarity with the sergeant.

The minutes ticked by endlessly as I fidgeted on the bench, my buttocks uncomfortably numb from their contact with the rigid surface. Since wild speculation did nothing to calm my frazzled nerves, I tried to control my thoughts. The sound of raised voices filtered through from the office: recognising the distinctive voice of the local undertaker, I was tempted to throw myself on the floor and offer up a prayer of thanks. Since the greasy looking linoleum didn't appear to have been intimate with a mop for the last couple of decades, I managed to restrain myself at the sound of heavy footsteps approaching.

The young policeman entered the cell. Ignoring me, he turned towards a row of lockers against one wall. Retrieving a Tupperware box from one of the lockers, he addressed me. "Sandwitch."

"No thank, you," I responded. "This place has rather made me lose my appetite. A coffee would be most welcome though."

"*Ti?*" he questioned, before barking an order. "Come."

I was relieved to see that he was heading back to the sergeant's office rather than leading me down to some dungeon. There was no sign of Spiros, making me wonder if I could perchance have simply imagined hearing his voice due to the stress of being incarcerated.

Drawing level with the sergeant's desk, the policeman barked, "Wait." Taking a seat, he began to tuck into the sandwich whilst I hovered nervously. I felt rather stupid: even when he had addressed me in English, I had managed to get the wrong end of the stick, presuming he had been offering me a sandwich when he had merely been collecting his own packed lunch from his locker.

Clocking the young policeman eating, the sergeant opined that he ought to find himself a wife who would pack him off to work with a proper lunch, like *pastitsio* or *moussaka*, rather than a boring sandwich. The young man rolled his eyes: I expect that he heard the same comment repeatedly.

"*I mama mou eftiaxe afto to santouits,*" the young policeman retorted, saying his mother had made the sandwich. Since he appeared to be deriving no enjoyment from the rather stale looking offering, I imagined that his mother shared the sergeant's opinion that it was high time he found a wife instead of living in the parental home. Before he could devour any more of the sandwich, the sergeant barked at him to go and tell the undertaker to come back in.

When Spiros bounced in, I must confess that I had never been so relieved to see anyone in my life.

"Victor," Spiros shouted, rushing forward to

embrace me.

"Spiro," I cried. Throwing myself into his embrace, I fought back the tears threatening to leak from my eyes, touched beyond measure that Spiros had wasted no time in rushing to my aid. He was not alone: Vangelis and Panos were with him.

Taking one look at me, Vangelis exclaimed, "Victor, what have they to done to you? I never to see you look so the rubbish. And the blood. Did the police to beat you?"

"No one has mistreated me," I assured him.

"We come to get you out," Spiros told me.

"I am so grateful," I gushed.

"But the sergeant say we have to wait until the Tina come," he added.

"The Athena has to gone with the Barry to show to him where the mother of the Tina live," Vangelis volunteered. I was instantly buoyed up to hear that my friends were rallying round to secure my release.

"*Irtha se periptosi pou chreiazontan ligo mi,*" Panos added. I burst into laughter at his ludicrous statement that he came along in case they needed some muscle: even so, it was good to know the burly farmer was in my corner and more than willing to give it a bit of welly.

"Kyria Kompogiannopoulou is here somewhere too," I said.

"They let her to go to the near taverna toilet. They to worry she to lecture them on the dirty state of the toilet here," Spiros revealed. "When the Nikos come, they to let him take the Kyria Kompogiannopoulou back to the Meli but you must to wait here until the Tina come."

"Nikos is on his way?" I said, surprised to hear that the taverna owner would soon be joining us.

"He is the behind us. I think the moped not to go as quick as the hearse." Lowering his voice to a whisper, Spiros added with a wink, "The Nikos to bring the *fakelaki*."

"I'm not sure that attempting to bribe me out of here is a good idea," I cautioned, worried that his mention of a brown envelope may result in my being escorted back to my cell. On reflection, I supposed that technically the room I had been told to wait in hadn't actually been a cell. Considering the young policeman kept his sandwiches there, I supposed it must be the staff room. In fairness, I had seen worse hovels serving as staff quarters in the catering trade during my illustrious career as a public health inspector.

"Niko," the sergeant shouted, rushing forward to greet the Meli taverna owner and plant a couple of kisses on his cheeks. I supposed that things must be looking up if Nikos was on kissing terms with the local constabulary. As my ex-employer as well as a close friend, it ought to carry some weight in my favour if Nikos vouched for me.

"Victor, I come as fast as I can," Nikos said, his strong embrace threatening to bruise my ribs. "I was to pick the olive with the Guzim when the old man who write the sex book tell me the police to take you away." Lowering his voice to a hiss, a smile creased his handsome features and his eyes twinkled as he added, "The Guzim think it best he not come to the *astynomiko tmima* with me, he not strictly legal. But he to put the first five *evro* in the *fakelaki* and he knock the door to collect the more cash for me to bring the here."

Once again the tears threatened to spill from my eyes at the thought that Guzim had not only arranged a whip round for a bribe but had been the first to contribute. Catching sight of the wad of notes, Spiros rushed over. Grabbing the envelope, he none too discreetly attempted to pass it to the sergeant. My heart dropped into my boots when the sergeant became visibly annoyed, announcing that he didn't accept brown envelopes. My worry that the sergeant would clap Spiros into handcuffs for attempting to bribe a policeman was allayed when Barry, Athena and Tina arrived, distracting the sergeant's attention before the situation could escalate.

"I couldn't believe it when I heard you'd been arrested," Barry cried, rushing forward to hug me.

"Vangeli, tell them in Greek that they'll never meet anyone more law abiding than Victor. Tell them that he's such a stickler for the rules that he won't even double park."

Whilst Vangelis bent the sergeant's ear by reeling off a long laundry list of all the rules that I, as an exemplary upstanding European citizen with Greek residency, would never dream of breaking, Tina grabbed my arm.

"Victor, I am the so sorry that the police to bring you here."

"I do hope that you've brought the permit for Sunday trading," I snapped, feeling not a whit of guilt that my response was a tad ungracious.

"No, I not to have one…"

"But you've been on the wrong side of the law before for trading without one," I exclaimed, hardly crediting that Tina could be so rash as to continue trading without permission after already being caught out.

"I am the sorry, Victor. I not expect to make you the trouble. The permit he is the difficult, so much the red tape to stamp," Tina sighed. "I never to think any the person would to report you."

"I've got a fair idea that it was your mother who alerted the police," I said.

"No. No I cannot to believe it," Tina protested.

"Think about it, Tina," I encouraged. "She is

spiteful enough to want to see me arrested as revenge for the way my tongue got the better of me this morning."

"She was very the angry, it is the true. But…no… she wouldn't…"

"What?" I prompted.

"It would to mean they might padlock the shop…"

"And if the shop is closed then you would be free to be at her beck and call again."

Clapping a hand in front of her mouth, Tina gasped. "My own mother…and after I stay at the hospital with her and bring her home to look after the knee…I think you are the right, Victor, but it pain me to say it."

Tina threw her hands in front of her face and began to weep, bemoaning the sacrifices she had made to be at her mother's bedside even though her efforts had been unappreciated. My first instinct was to wonder if it may be a cunning womanly ploy to turn the waterworks on to win sympathy from the policemen, but it appeared that Tina's tears were genuine. It had finally dawned on her that Despina was a thoroughly nasty piece of work, so spiteful and vengeful that she was willing to risk the closure of her daughter's business to pay me back for spewing a few home truths. The sergeant was clearly embarrassed; I supposed that the criminal class he was used to dealing with didn't make a habit of blubbing all over his office.

Clearly desperate to wrap up the business of illegal Sunday trading and get shut of the lot of us, the sergeant invited Tina to take the seat in front of his desk. As the sergeant interrogated Tina about her wilful breach of the law in trading without the requisite Sunday permit, I found it difficult to follow what Tina was saying in Greek, her words rather distorted as she alternated between hiccupping and sobbing. She appeared to be laying the excuses on with a trowel, pulling out the sympathy card as she explained that being forced to care for her old fragile mother left her no time to run around visiting fifty different offices in order to obtain all the rubber stamps needed to secure the permit.

"Tina tell that she ask the you and the Kyria Sofia to look after the shop because she lose so much the money by closing when the Despina was in the hospital," Vangelis helpfully translated for my benefit. "She beg the police to not to padlock the shop, she promise to get the permit."

"*Entaxei*," the sergeant said wearily. "*Den tha kleisoume to katistima sas, alla prepei na plirosete prostimo.*"

"I didn't follow that," I hissed to Vangelis.

"He say okay, he not to close the shop but she must to pay the fine."

"*Alla den echo chrimata giati frontizo tin arrosti gria mou,*" Tina cried.

"She say…" Vangelis began.

"It's okay, Vangeli, I understood that she said she has no money because she has been looking after her old sick mother."

"*Bravo*, Victor. Your Greek is to the much improve," Vangelis said.

"*Mou eipe oti den katalave kanena Elliniko,*" the young policemen said, staring at me suspiciously as he told Vangelis that I had said I didn't understand any Greek.

"*Den katalavaino,*" I replied innocently, emboldened by the presence of my friends.

As Tina continued her lament about being penniless, Nikos stepped forward, suggesting that they use the money collected from my whip-round to pay a bribe, to instead pay Tina's fine.

"Everyone to lose if the shop to be padlock because the Tina cannot to pay," Nikos reasoned.

"*Prepei na kano ti grafiki ergasia.*" Groaning heavily, the sergeant announced he must do the paperwork. Realising that his office was a tad cluttered with Meli villagers, he pointed at me and Tina. "*Esy kai esy, meine. Ola ta ypoloipa pigainoun.*"

"He to say you and Tina to stay, all the rest to go," Spiros helpfully translated. "I will to tell him I will to stay with the you, Victor, to help the translate and take you home."

As the sergeant began the laborious job of completing the paperwork, the rest of the villagers left, Nikos saying he would take Kyria Sofia back to Meli on the back of his moped. Barry was reluctant to leave me but Spiros assured him we would soon be following in short order. His estimation proved a tad optimistic: it took the best part of two hours before we were formally free to go, the sergeant slowly typing up his report using just one rather than the proverbial two fingers, shouting out to the young policeman to give him a hand with the computer when it all got a tad too confusing.

I must confess to being rather taken aback when Spiros informed me that I must pay a fine, though it was nowhere near as hefty as Tina's. They both insisted on handing over the cash collected from the villagers for a bribe on my behalf, but as Tina was left out of pocket she couldn't afford to pay my wage for the day, instead palming me off later with a choice selection of dented tins and some produce that was perilously close to its sell-by-date.

"It's bad enough that everyone else teases me endlessly about being arrested, but I expected better of you, Barry," I chided as he made the observation that the police had missed a trick that day by not making me pose for a mug shot.

"I can just picture your photo staring down from the wall of the police station," Barry snorted. "Unshaven with blood shot eyes, wearing that blood stained apron and wielding a meat cleaver."

I deduced from Marigold's expression of fury that she wouldn't be averse to taking a meat cleaver to her beloved brother at that moment.

"Enough, Barry. I don't want to hear another word about Victor's unfortunate brush with the law. Once and for all, he does not have a criminal record…"

"Only because the fine was paid. I contributed a tenner myself, you know," Barry reminded us.

I reflected that at least one good thing had come out of it all. The way in which the villagers had rallied round to secure my release either by showing up at the police station in person or by contributing to the brown envelope, showed that I was a valued member of the community.

"But that beard really must go. I want my clean shaven husband back," Marigold insisted.

"But when you first got home from Manchester, you said that my beard gave me a distinguished air," I reminded her.

"That was before you told me about your run in with the law. Ever since you came clean, I can't help associating your facial growth with the type of undesirable that ends up serving time, especially when your mother insists on reminding me about your criminal lineage on your paternal side."

Chapter 5

Violet Burke's Blocked Toilet

Strolling home from Barry's shed, Marigold linked her arm in mine. "It's supposed to be a full moon tonight. It will add a touch of romance when we make our way home from Doreen's later."

"Very romantic with my mother in tow," I chortled.

"Do pop in on her now, darling. Tell her that we'll collect her at 7pm to go over to Doreen's together. I don't like to think of your mother walking the streets of Meli alone in the dark."

Biting back my witty retort that it was unlikely

anyone would mistake Violet Burke for a street walker, I settled instead for saying, "If she's home. She might still be up to her neck peeling potatoes in the taverna."

"Well Cynthia's bicycle is outside the door...oh, good grief. What on earth has your mother done to the saddle?" Marigold exclaimed.

Whipping a torch from my pocket, the beam illuminated a garish new addition resembling a crocheted tea cosy fashioned from a mix of clashing lime green and bright pink wool.

"It looks as though Violet Burke has cobbled together a buttock protector," I laughed. "You know how she's always complaining how uncomfortable the saddle is..."

"Though her choice of phrase is certainly more vulgar," Marigold reminded me. "Now, don't let her keep you gassing all day. Make sure you leave enough time to shave that fluff off your chin."

"I won't be long," I promised. "Pop the outside lights on when you get upstairs. I need to look in on the chickens before I part with my goatee."

As Marigold tripped upstairs, the *apothiki* door was flung open by a balaclava clad bulbous figure padded out to gargantuan proportions by a Puffa jacket. The only hint that it was Violet Burke rather than a home invader attempting to mask their identity was the carping complaint that greeted me:

"There you are at last, Victor. I've been looking everywhere for you."

"Why are you wearing a balaclava indoors?" I
asked.

"I had it on under my cycling helmet. It keeps
my complexion from getting all ruddy and chapped
in the wind," she explained, pulling the balaclava
off to reveal a shock of vermilion mussed hair. Considering the patchy application of the dye, I presumed that my mother must have resorted to col-
ouring her coiffure in the sink rather than being
professionally ministered to in Athena's kitchen.

"Aren't you a tad overheated in that bulky
jacket?" I asked.

"Give me chance to take it off, lad. I've only
been home five minutes." I couldn't help but smile
inwardly to hear my mother referring to the *apothiki*
as home: it was less than a month since she made
the move to Greece, a major upheaval considering
her age. "I had to go out and scrounge a plunger
from Athena…"

"I have a plunger upstairs that you could have
borrowed, Mother."

"Could have if you'd been at home to give me
a lend," Vi pointed out. "There was no time to hang
about waiting for you, not when I saw the state my
toilet was in when I got home from the taverna."

"How many times must I remind you that you

can't go flushing toilet paper down the loo?" I cried in exasperation at my mother's failure to follow the Greek toilet rule. "The pipes just aren't designed for it, they're much too narrow. You have to put your used toilet roll in the bin to avoid a blockage."

"It's a filthy habit that I can't get my head round, lad," Vi grimaced in disgust. "It's just plain nasty having a bin full of used bog roll stinking out the bathroom."

"I would imagine that your blocked toilet stinks a darn sight more," I pointed out.

"Aye, that it does," she conceded. "It's a good job you didn't have the bathroom done out with carpet. There was horrible sludgy stuff overflowing all over the floor. Anyway, I couldn't hang around waiting for you to turn up with a plunger and I thought Athena would have one handy, what with her husband being a builder."

"But how did you manage to communicate with her?"

"I called round and dragged her into the lav and mimed unblocking it."

It was a relief to hear that she hadn't demonstrated a blockage by throwing loo roll down Athena's toilet in order to get her point across.

"So, did you manage to get your hands on a plunger?" I asked with a sinking feeling, realising that at any moment my mother might start

demanding that I unblock her toilet. I had no appetite for such an unpleasant task just prior to being
expected to choke down Norman's experimental
cooking. "It's probably best if I telephone Barry and
get him to come over to sort it. That reminds me,
Barry will be your plus one for this evening's expat
dinner party."

"It's a good job you told me now," Vi said. "I
was just about to ask young Theo if he fancied coming with me."

"Who on earth is Theo?"

"That Jehovah's Witness what is busy unclog-
ging the lav."

"You've lost me, Mother."

"I'd just got home with the plunger when luckily that nice young man that has been trying to convert me came knocking. It turns out that he's a dab
hand with my backed up pipes."

"Mother, you can't just go round inviting random unknowns in to take care of your plumbing
needs," I said, exasperated by her recklessness. This
so-called Jehovah's Witness could well be a fraud
looking to take advantage of vulnerable pensioners
with the aim of robbing them blind.

"Get a grip, Victor. What do you think the puny
lad is going to do? Beat me to death with the toilet
plunger before legging it with my chip pan and hot
water bottle," Violet Burke spat. "Anyway, Theo is

not that random. He's stopped by a couple of times now for a chat. It's nice to have someone local that speaks English, and remember, he brought me that book a few weeks ago?"

"He brought you a Bible, Mother," I said, coming up blank as I tried to recall if I had ever run into Violet Burke's Jehovah's Witness.

"Well, he spouts a bit of religious guff but it's mainly just to keep up appearances. His heart's not in it, you can tell. He knows that I come from a long line of Methodists. Enos Blossom was quite big in the local chapter..." Violet Burke stopped mid-sentence, overcome with a fit of coughing.

Beyond confused, I pondered why it never seemed possible to have a simple conversation with my mother without her chequered past being dragged into it. About to sarcastically ask if Enos Blossom was yet another in the long line of my mother's discarded husbands, she managed to bring her coughing under control.

"All that biking has taken the wind out of me, Victor. Now, as I was saying, Enos Blossom was big in the local Methodist chapter back in the century before the last one, so young Theo knows he hasn't got a cat's chance of turning me into one of them Witnesses. I've had my fill of the God squad and no mistake. I think he's just a bit lonely, like. He's not had it easy, poor love."

BUCKET TO GREECE (VOL.10)

Mother's reference to the nineteenth century made me recall that Enos Blossom had actually been Violet Burke's grandfather. I remembered her telling me that he had been one of the original divers on the Manchester ship canal. I was glad that I hadn't accused her of divorcing a relative but her words made me curious about her young visitor.

"I'm still not happy about you inviting a stranger in, Mother," I cautioned.

"He's not a stranger to me. Come through to the bathroom and meet him if it will put your mind at rest," she invited.

Fortunately I was spared from slopping around in Violet Burke's overflowed sewage when the young man in question stuck his head around the living room door. "Do you have a, *pos to les*?" the young man finished his sentence with 'How to say?'

"What are you saying, lad? You know I don't understand a word of Greek," Violet Burke said, her regular bark tempered with a note of affection.

"I try to think the English word for the *sfoungaristra kai kouva*," he said shyly.

"A mop and bucket," I helpfully translated.

"It's in the kitchen," Vi told him. "But don't go trailing any muck from the bathroom in there. I only gave it a good bottoming this morning."

"Bottoming?" the young man repeated.

"Never mind, I'll fetch the mop," I offered.

"And I'll put the kettle on for a nice cup of tea," Vi said.

"The foreign tea in the bag?" Theo asked, his guile free eyes lighting up with enthusiasm.

"That's right, lad. You won't be getting any of that mucky stuff with twigs floating round in it when you have a cuppa here."

"I do wish that you would stop referring to *tsai tou vounou* as mucky stuff. You might end up causing offence to your new Greek friends," I sighed.

"Piffle. They can't understand a word that I say," Vi pointed out, ever the pragmatist.

Taking a closer look at the young man, I couldn't recall seeing him before in the area though clearly he seemed to be on quite familiar terms with my mother. I reflected that he would be hard to miss in Meli where the average age of the residents was eighty: he would be sure to stand out by virtue of his extreme youth. Tall and lanky, he didn't appear to be a day over twenty, though his facial features were somewhat obscured by an overly long and foppish fringe flopping over his pale face.

"So, Theo, my mother tells me that you live locally," I said, hoping to elicit some information.

"I am rent the small cottage in Nektar for six weeks now," Theo volunteered in excellent English. "When I was allowed to leave Athens, I wanted to find a quiet place far away to recover…"

"Have you been ill?" I asked.

"No, I mean to recover from the stress of enduring life in the city. I needed somewhere peaceful to find myself."

I was a tad confused by his remark: mother had given me the impression that he was a religious zealot but he was coming across as a New Age hippie.

"When you say you were allowed to leave Athens…were you being held there against your will?" It struck me that was the politest way of asking if he had been recently incarcerated. It wouldn't do to have my mother mixing with newly released ex-criminals after all the bother I'd gone to in getting her away from the dreadful Billings clan back in Warrington.

"I clean and tell you at the same time," Theo said, carrying the mop bucket through to the bathroom where he immediately got stuck in mopping up the disgusting effluent. I was keen to hear what he had to say: if nothing else, his skill with the mop proved that he wasn't a work-shy shirker.

"I was not in the prison, though I would have been if they had not to change the law only a few years ago. Until 1997 the government sent the conscientious objectors to prison when they refuse to do the military service. My two elder brothers serve the prison time for their conscience and my father before them."

"I do believe that I've read something about that," I said, thinking it was like something out of the dark ages to imprison those unable to fulfil their mandatory military service due to strongly held religious beliefs. Greece is after all part of the European Union rather than some dodgy third-world hellhole under the rule of a dictator.

"The Greece law change in 1997. Since then, the conscientious objector is required to serve the fifteen months in alternate service to the military."

"But I thought conscripts only served nine months," I said, recalling the subject being discussed in the taverna amongst my Greek friends. They were very vocal on the topic since back in the day the old-timers had been called up to do a couple of years: in comparison, they thought that the youngsters of today got off lightly with less than a year.

"The conscription is the nine months but the alternate service is double," Theo explained. "They make it very difficult on the purpose. They not allow the alternate service to be done close to home yet they not to pay enough to cover the housing."

"What did this alternate service involve?" I asked.

"I had to work as the orderly in a state hospital in Athens. I not like the big city and it was the expensive to live. The pay was so low I could barely survive and the family little money to help."

"Where is your family from?"

"Lamia, but I not want to return to the family. When I to leave Athens, I have much confusion." Lowering his voice, he confided, "I have doubts about my religion."

"How so?"

"In Athens the kind woman find me sleeping rough in the park. I tell her my circumstance and she invite me to live in her house. I only pay little the rent. She was good to me, but when I tell my family they say this is wrong, it is wrong to make the good kind friend if she is not a Witness. I tell them she is the good Orthodox woman but still they say it goes against our teachings. My religion discourages any relationships outside our church, but it is was not easy to sleep outside in winter and I was weak."

I could only imagine how Theo's family would have a downer if they discovered he had been fraternising with the likes of Violet Burke.

"And then the Kyria who let me to live in her home became ill and I take her to the hospital. They say without the blood transfusion she will die. My religion teach the blood transfusion is wrong but it is more wrong in my mind to let the kind woman die. It make me to question my faith in a religion that tells me it is wrong to have an innocent friend-ship with an outsider who should be left to die be-cause the transfused blood is prohibited. So I move away to reflect on these things, away from the in-fluence of other Witnesses."

"But you're still hoping to do a spot of convert-ing by giving out Bibles," I pointed out.

"My heart is not in it," Theo said with a heart-felt sigh. "I do it for the chance to make some com-pany, I am shy to make friends. When I meet your mother, she is so kind. She make the cup of tea and make the chat, and I can to practice my English with her."

"Your English is excellent," I assured him. "So how are you making a living now?"

"I have work the olive harvest in Nektar. I not need much. I want to live the simple life, to be at one with nature and grow my own food. Perhaps, I make the safe place for the others who question the religion we are brought up in."

To my mind, it sounded as though he was hop-ing to establish a self-sufficient commune for ex-Witnesses. It would certainly introduce some wel-come new young blood to the area. I imagined that as long as they kept a lid on any proselytising, they would be made welcome by the locals though it was anyone's guess how Papas Andreas would react. He may well consider a rival religion competition even if its proponents were lapsed.

A couple of flushes demonstrated that Violet Burke's toilet was as good as new. Theo, not wishing to intrude, prepared to take his leave, refusing to accept any payment for ministering to my mother's lavatory. It appeared that Violet Burke was a pretty good judge of character after all.

"I'll put in a good word for you with that Doreen woman later," my mother told Theo as he departed, weighed down by the generous gift of the deep fat fryer that Violet Burke had turned her nose up at when Marigold bought it.

"That Doreen needs a hand getting her garden mulched," my mother explained as we waved Theo off. "You could put a bit of work his way in your garden. 'Appen he might look puny but he's got a good work ethic. Not to mention he's a sight more presentable than that shifty Albanian what's always flashing his bits in your garden."

"Tempting though it is, Mother, I'm rather afraid that I'm stuck with Guzim for the foreseeable."

Chapter 6

Unwelcome Visitors

Leaving the *apothiki*, I braced myself against the cold nip in the early December air, shivers fluttering down my spine as the chilly breeze slapped the back of my neck. At least the contentious goatee was finally serving its purpose of acting as a serviceable chin warmer. It was Sod's law that after several weeks of careful cultivation, Marigold was now insisting I rid myself of the beard just when it was turning out to have some practical purpose.

Striding through the garden to check on the chickens, I nearly jumped out of my skin when

BUCKET TO GREECE (VOL.10)

Guzim popped out from behind the orange tree with no warning. One would think by now, I ought to have become accustomed to his serial habit of lurking in my garden. The rapidly waning beam from my torch settled on Guzim, the dim glow highlighting his own attempts to cultivate a beard. His efforts were decidedly peculiar, the hairy growth extending well below his chin to cover the entirety of his neck, transforming him into a veritable werewolf, albeit a scrawny one. Since his beard had been sparser than mine only a couple of days earlier, I jumped to the natural assumption that he was taking some dodgy drug to encourage a spurt of unnatural hair growth.

It was only when the hair on the Albanian shed dweller's neck began to move on its own volition that I realised that it wasn't actually attached to him: he had wrapped his blasted pet rabbit around his scruff, seemingly using the tame animal as a makeshift scarf. Much as Marigold may be amused if I shared Guzim's latest quirk with her, I didn't want my wife getting any ideas about incorporating our imported domestics into her winter wardrobe. I suppose on reflection that it would be most unlikely that Marigold would take fashion tips from the grubby Albanian or that using pets as fashion accessories would ever catch on.

"*Evala ta kotopoula kato gia ti nychta,*" Guzim

said, informing me that he had put the chickens down for the night.

When I mentioned that it was a tad early for the poultry to be bedding down, my gardener explained he had plans for the evening. Although I waited with bated breath for him to elaborate, no further information was forthcoming; sparking my curiosity to what Guzim was up to. Since Nikos discouraged him from sitting around taking up valuable space nursing a single bottle of Amstel for hours on end whilst complaining that his wife in Albania ate all his money, Guzim rarely made an appearance in the taverna. It struck me that I had little idea how Guzim actually occupied his free time: it must be a solitary existence in the pink palace of love with only Doruntina for company. Perhaps realising that I was waiting to have my curiosity satisfied, Guzim moved closer and hissed in my ear, *"Tha sou po avrio,"* meaning he would tell me tomorrow. Lowering his voice to barely a whisper, he added that he did not want to tell me his plans in front of the rabbit as Doruntina was keenly sensitive.

"To pairno to Alvaniko kouneli katalavainei ta Ellinika tote," I retorted sarcastically, saying I took it that the Albanian rabbit understood Greek then.

When Guzim responded with an emphatic *"Vevaios,"* meaning certainly, I realised my sarcasm was lost on him. Turning on his heel, the Albanian

shed dweller scurried off through my garden towards the street, the apparently sensitive rabbit still
clinging on limpet-like to his neck. My mind boggled; Guzim was clearly delusional enough to believe that his Albanian bred rabbit could compre-
hend Greek. I was rather looking forward to way-
laying my gardener the next day and grilling him
about his night on the town with his bunny companion. If nothing else, it may serve as an amusing
anecdote.

Entering the house, I called out to my wife,
"Marigold, you won't believe this. Violet Burke has
only roped in some random Jehovah's Witness to
unblock her toilet…"

Walking into the grand salon, the words froze
on my lips when I discovered a vaguely familiar
looking couple in the company of my wife, Marigold bearing a marked resemblance to a startled
deer caught in the headlights.

"Victor, there you are, darling. Now, you do remember Emily and Bill," Marigold prompted me,
firing a look of desperation in my direction.

"Umm…" At a complete loss, I tried to place
the couple, wondering if perchance we had run into
them at the market or perhaps in Lidl, Marigold
having the indiscriminate habit of stopping to chat
with anyone that her radar identified as English.
Able to detect fellow expats at fifty paces, my wife

would think nothing of stopping to ambush them by blocking their way with her shopping trolley to compare experiences about living abroad.

"They were waiting on the doorstep when I got back from Barry's," Marigold said, slapping a fake smile on her face.

"Good to see you again, Vincent." The paunchy man extended his hand in greeting. I noticed that his wife resembled a nodding dog, her head dipping up and down perhaps to counter her fixed immobile expression. In contrast, the man's jowls had a discernible wobble. Being rather on the slack side, his double chins complemented his prominent paunch.

"It's Victor…" I corrected.

"Good of you and Margaret to insist that we break up our tour by staying here. Hotels can be so impersonal, nothing like a bit of home comfort and the chance to catch up with old neighbours. I said to Emily, fancy Vincent and Margaret moving abroad. I wouldn't have pegged you as the get-up-and-go types flitting to foreign parts. I said to Emily, it takes all types."

"It's Marigold. Victor and Marigold…" my wife interjected, her words echoed a second later by Emily.

Their words fell on deaf ears as the paunchy fellow steamrollered on without pausing for breath.

BUCKET TO GREECE (VOL.10)

"I would have had you down as the sort to spend your retirement running the neighbourhood watch and mowing the lawn. It takes all types, I said to Emily, didn't I?"

"Bill was chuffed to bits when I told him that you'd moved to Greece," Emily piped up. "He'd been worried about having to compete with you for the role of Coordinator of the Neighbourhood Watch when he retired. With you out of the picture, the committee practically gobbled him up."

Not only was I at a complete loss to place this pair of random oddballs who had apparently flown over to Greece for a freeloading holiday with a couple called Vincent and Margaret, but I was baffled by the very suggestion that coordinating a neighbourhood watch group would ever appeal to me. Whilst I have nothing against such schemes per se, I would run a mile before involving myself with a bunch of nosy curtain-twitchers with nothing better to do than spy on their neighbours.

"Marigold, a word," I said, gesticulating towards the kitchen.

"If you'll just excuse us a second…" Marigold said to the pair. Seemingly oblivious to our departure, Bill carried on pontificating whilst Emily continued her imitation of a nodding dog.

"Oh, Victor, I'm sorry to spring them on you like this…" Marigold hissed, her voice barely above a whisper as we huddled just out of earshot beside the fridge.

"Who on earth are they?" I was genuinely clueless.

"Emily and Bill. They lived three doors down to us in Manchester, you must remember them."

"Ah…I knew I'd seen him before but I'm pretty certain I've never actually spoken to him. Just the occasional wave when we headed out to work or when he was washing his car. Do you actually know him?"

"Not really, though I did take a parcel in for him once. I had the odd coffee with Emily…"

"Well, what's all this guff about you inviting them over for a holiday?"

"I didn't. Well, not exactly. Remember that I told you that I ran into Emily when I went over to stay with Geraldine and I told her about our move to Greece."

I had a vague recollection about Marigold mentioning it when she'd phoned me from Manchester.

"Well, we've exchanged the odd email since I got back. Emily was keen to keep in touch as they were planning a tour of the Peloponnese. I may have said come and stay for the night if you're in the area."

"So, you did invite them?"

"Well, sort of. I was going to mention it nearer

the time…I know how cranky you can get about houseguests."

"Nearer the time?" I queried, ignoring Marigold's slur implying I was inhospitable.

"They weren't due until Thursday."

"It is Thursday," I pointed out in exasperation.

"I mean next Thursday…I was rather taken aback when I got home and discovered them on the doorstep with their suitcases. It must be a case of crossed wires."

My heart plummeted. It dawned on me that this pair of randoms wasn't so random after all; the chances that it was Marigold who got her wires crossed appeared highly likely.

"What do you think we should do with them? We're supposed to be having dinner at Doreen's shortly. Do you suppose Doreen could squeeze them in? It will play havoc with her seating plan."

"Doreen's dinner party is the least of it," I pointed out. "Are we seriously expected to give house room to a couple of strangers?"

"Well, strictly speaking they aren't technically strangers. Like I said, we've exchanged the odd email and are on slightly more than nodding terms," Marigold argued.

"Speaking of nodding, what's that all about?" I asked, gesticulating towards the grand salon with my head. "That Emily person has the most peculiar way of nodding yet her expression is utterly fixed."

"I think Emily must have had Botox, I could swear her face used to have more wrinkles." Adopting a wheedling tone, Marigold said, "We can hardly turn them out now in the dark. Where would they go?"

"They can drive down to the coast. I'm sure there must still be a couple of hotels open at this time of year," I suggested.

"But I already offered them a bed for the night," Marigold blurted.

As I opened my mouth to object, Marigold pre-empted my protestations by fluttering her eyelashes at me, admitting, "It's just for one night and I didn't know what else to do with them. It would be terribly ill-mannered to rescind the invitation now that I've said they can stay."

Presented with a fait accompli, I realised that I could hardly kick the pair out now that they had managed to put one over on Marigold by worming their way into our spare bedroom.

"One night, Marigold," I conceded, bracing myself to make small talk with a couple of strangers.

Re-joining the interlopers, I noticed that Emily and Bill looked a tad awkward. I imagined that it had perhaps belatedly dawned on them that we hadn't been expecting them. I wondered if they intended to bluff it out.

Pre-empting me, Emily said, "We seem to have caught you off-guard so I pulled out the email. I printed everything off before we left Manchester. Look, it's all arranged with Marigold to spend the night here before we continue on to Sparta…"

"Sparta."

"Yes, it's all on our itinerary. We took the circuitous route to call on you since Emily said Marigold was so keen for us to see where you'd settled."

Perusing the printed paper which Bill shoved under my nose, I realised my wife had indeed dropped a clanger. There was no denying that an invitation had been extended: Marigold's gushing insistence that they break up their journey was undeniably there in black and white. Putting myself in our visitor's shoes, I felt suitably mortified.

"We went out of our way to make the detour. There was a more direct route to Sparta," Bill insisted.

"Bill took a bit of persuading to make the detour…" Emily said. "I suppose the sight of our cases made you think that we'd landed on you for the duration. It's just that Bill doesn't like to risk leaving our valuables in the car."

"Can't be too careful, that's what I always say, isn't it Emily."

"You do, dear. Can't be too careful."

Whilst Marigold rustled up a pot of tea, I overcompensated for my initially inhospitable reception of the pair by listening with interest as Bill took me through their detailed tour itinerary, surprised that he had mapped out a route off the usual tourist trail, incorporating overnight stays at Sparta and Monemvasia. He explained that he preferred to explore out of season when the place wasn't overrun with tourists and he didn't need to worry about suffering intolerable heat and mosquitoes. Appreciating Bill's meticulous road plan and his keen research into the area, I mellowed towards him, offering a few pointers on places of interest that they may care to explore.

Marigold finally took the bull by the horns, reddening as she admitted that she had cocked the dates up and hadn't actually been expecting them until next week. Confessing that we had a prior engagement, Bill and Emily took it surprisingly well. Declining Marigold's offer to see if Doreen could squeeze an extra couple of chairs around the table, the couple implored us not to change our plans on their account, insisting they were too tired after all the driving to venture out again. A compromise was reached whereby they would spend the night in our guest bedroom and the next day they would break up their journey to Sparta by stopping in Itilo where we would join them for lunch. As I mulled that a bed for the night and a slap-up lunch at my expense was a small price to pay for Marigold's cock-up, I realised that I had tuned out and Bill was once again chuntering on about the neighbourhood watch.

"Sorry, I didn't quite catch that," I said.

"I was saying that the way that you just upped and sold your house like that prompted the neighbourhood watch committee to try and push through new guidelines…"

"You've rather lost me," I said, wondering what the sale of our Manchester house over two years ago had to do with anything.

"We've been trying to get a petition going to say that residents of the Close can't just sell to anyone. We'd like to be able to vet new buyers and put them to a vote."

"I'm pretty sure that's actually illegal," I pointed out.

"Then the law is an ass and needs changing," Bill blustered. "Selling your house to that dreadful builder chap really lowered the tone: it simply wasn't fair to expect the other residents of the Close to live in such forced proximity to him."

Casting my mind back, I tried to recall the buyer who had purchased our Manchester home. Though most of the viewings had been done through the estate agent whilst we had been house hunting in the Mani, I recalled meeting the buyer, a bumptious builder called Gary. I had been busy packing the house up for the move when Gary dropped in with his damp meter. Beyond his mention of an allergy to cats, not much else sprang to mind.

"I didn't meet the buyer, but Victor did," Marigold said. Turning to me, she added, "That evening when we had our farewell dinner at the Bhilai Bhaji with Benjamin and Adam, you told us the buyer had called round. I'm sure you would have mentioned any red flags if you'd noticed anything odd about him."

Mention of our favourite Indian restaurant reminded me that Gary had told me that he'd been partial to a takeaway vindaloo from the Spice Bucket, a particularly grubby establishment on my inspection patch. It had only been professional restraint that prevented me from warning Gary about the wisdom of eating anything that emanated from their kitchen. I was well acquainted with their lax hygiene standards, having only grudgingly awarded the Spice Bucket a reluctant number one on the Food Standards Agency hygiene scoreboard.

The conversation I'd had with Gary as he'd prostrated himself next to the skirting board came back to me: he had questioned the wisdom of our up-sticking to Greece. Apparently he had no truck with travelling abroad, rather disconcerted by the notion of eating foreign food in hot climates. Ironically, he considered the salmonella laden offerings from the Indian kitchen of the Spice Bucket to be the best of British cuisine.

"I remember Gary wasn't too keen on abroad but that's hardly a reason to suppose that he wouldn't fit into the neighbourhood," I said.

"But that tatty old van of his stands out as decidedly common," Bill said, his accusatory tone suggesting that I was personally responsible for the house buyer's choice of transport. "It was only professionals in the Close until you sold your house to a boorish tradesman."

"That sounds like a sweeping generalisation; I certainly didn't have a clue what most of the neighbours did for a living." The area had certainly been a respectable one to hang up my hat at the end of a long day of sanitary inspections, but since most people had kept to themselves it had lacked the close neighbourhood vibe which we enjoyed in Meli

"Well, what was your front garden now looks more like a scrap yard. Full of cement mixers and wheelbarrows," Bill complained.

"And Gary has the most common relatives…" Emily joined in.

"A real motley crew," Bill confirmed.

"I didn't meet his wife though Gary did mention

that she quite fancied taking a holiday in Spain," I said. "Although he wasn't keen on the idea of foreign travel, I hardly think that marks him out as a persona non grata."

"I see that you've picked up a bit of the foreign lingo living here," Emily said, her expressionless face leading me to believe she was serious. Unable to resist winding her up, I kept my face as straight as Emily's as I retorted, "Yes, they're very big on Latin in Greece."

Our unwanted guests exchanged a confused look, my little quip flying over their heads.

"Gary's wife did go out to Spain not long after they moved in. You'll never guess, she only went and did a Shirley Valentine," Emily revealed, her immovable face belying the satisfaction she appeared to derive from spreading a juicy piece of gossip.

"She ran off with a Greek fisherman in Spain?" Marigold said, biting her lower lip in an effort to try and conceal her amusement. I noticed that my wife's face was delightfully expressive in contrast to Emily's stiff features.

"No, the builder's wife took up with some Brit who'd moved out there," Emily said. "She showed me his picture when she came back to pack up her things, he was all hairy beer belly and dangling gold chains. I expect he was one of those Brits who moved to the Costa del Crime with his ill-gotten gains to avoid being extradited."

Not bothering to hide my sarcasm, I observed, "So, if the builder's wife ran off with another man, surely that was one less awful relative of Gary's for you to worry about."

"Oh, she wasn't too bad. At least it was only garden gnomes rather than concrete mixers before she left him, wasn't it Bill?" Emily said.

"She did have those questionable phallic garden statues," Bill reminded his wife.

"But they could be interpreted as artistic," Emily argued.

"I beg to differ. I found them as vulgar as some of the riff-raff that Gary has hanging round at his house," Bill said, shaking his head as though to dislodge some hideous memory.

"Bill's talking about this horrible old harridan who made a habit of turning up and creating such a scene. She was dreadfully common. Mutton dressed as lamb, had a bit of the Elsie Tanner about her…" Emily said.

"More of the Ena Sharples, I'd say," Bill interrupted. "She was loud and bolshie, quite intimidating."

"Anyway, she refused to shift from Gary's doorstep, didn't she Bill? She insisted that she was his mother, but he wasn't having any of it."

"She had a voice like a foghorn, it certainly carried," Bill hurriedly butted in as though to excuse their patent eavesdropping on Gary's private business.

"Can you imagine the inhumanity of someone denying their own mother?" Emily posited. Her attempt to raise her eyebrows failed miserably, making me think that Marigold must be onto something with her Botox theory.

"Can't say I blame him, he was probably hoping to get shot of the nutty old bat before someone called the police on her," Bill opined. "I shouldn't think Gary wanted the police poking round...you know what builders can be like for doing a bit of cash in hand."

"Surely it would be the Inland Revenue that he wouldn't want looking too closely..." Marigold pointed out, attempting to steer their line of chat away from all mention of an inconvenient relative turning up like a bolt from the blue. My wife had clearly cottoned on that Gary's embarrassing relative had been none other than Violet Burke. I remembered what a shock it had been when Gary telephoned me from Manchester to warn me about the persistent pensioner that had been pestering him relentlessly. Naturally she was nothing to do with him: Gary had a mother of his own who had been off enjoying the Illuminations in Blackpool when

Violet Burke had taken to stalking him, becoming an immovable feature in his front porch.

"But she told him straight that she'd traced him through the Salvation Army. Even though Gary is terribly common, he didn't want anything to do with the deranged old harridan," Bill elaborated. "Still, making a public display of washing his hands of his horrible old mother did nothing to endear Gary to the neighbours."

"We'd all seen the sort of vulgar stock he came from," Emily added.

Although I had jumped to the same conclusion about vulgar stock when Violet Burke had first landed on us in Meli, I resented the way that this gossiping pair so freely passed judgement on my mother. Although I had somewhat mellowed towards Bill, I found myself rapidly going off him again. Whilst I had finally come to terms with being abandoned in a bucket at the railway station and made peace with my absconded parent, I had no intention of revealing my ignominious start in life to Emily and Bill, or of offering up fodder for their idle gossip. Fortunately Marigold, having no desire to wash our dirty laundry in public, reminded me that I needed to shave quickly or we would be late for Doreen.

Dragging me through to the kitchen where I grudgingly unearthed a bottle of dubious plastic plonk for our visitors, Marigold hissed, "We need to get rid of them first thing before they clap eyes on your mother and put two and two together."

"That's a given," I agreed before suggesting, "Perhaps you should go to Doreen's on your own."

"She'd never forgive you if you bodged up her seating plan..."

"Well, I'm not too thrilled at the prospect of venturing out for the evening and leaving these practical strangers in our home," I protested.

"Oh Victor, I'm sure they are a perfectly respectable couple. After all, he's big in the neighbourhood watch. I very much doubt they intend to use their hire car as a getaway vehicle to make off with all our belongings."

Chapter 7

Anyone for Olives?

W hilst I'd busied myself lathering up and shaving off my carefully cultivated beard, Marigold had felt obliged to sit around making idle chit-chat with our unwanted visitors, leaving her no time to change her frock or primp and preen for the dinner party. Since we were running late, she was forced to settle for blasting her Titian tresses with a quick spritz of industrial strength hairspray.

"It doesn't matter what you look like, darling. It's only an expat dinner," I assured her. Intercepting her scathing look, I belatedly realised I'd gone and put my foot in it. Hoping to get back into my wife's good graces, I hastily tacked on a fawning compliment. "But you look as lovely as always, darling."

As Marigold's steely look melted, she ran an appreciative hand over my clean shaven face, her fingers lingering for a moment on my stubble free jaw. "Promise me you won't grow another one."

Heading down to the *apothiki* to collect Violet Burke, Marigold gasped as she recollected, "Oh no, I've just remembered that your mother is due to give our kitchen a good bottoming in the morning. What if Emily and Bill recognise her?"

"Let me think on it," I said, realising that loose lips could end up spreading my private business if Emily and Bill drew conclusions about why Gary in Manchester's distinctively unique and unforgettable mother was cleaning our house. Even though my mother was as keen as I was that no word of her abandoning me in a bucket ever got out, I could hardly rely on her to disown me in my own kitchen.

As Violet Burke joined us, wrapped up against the cold in the unflattering Puffa jacket and once again unrecognisable beneath her balaclava, I assured Marigold, "I told you there was no need to dress up," instantly losing all the brownie points bought by my earlier compliment.

Although Barry's smirk as he joined us suggested

he was amused by my mother's choice of headgear, he wisely kept his own counsel. Making our way through the village, our intended brisk progress was impeded by the plodding pace necessitated by Violet Burke's swollen feet. As she grumbled about the likelihood of her feet exploding, Barry offered a supportive arm. In no time at all the grin was wiped off his face as he was forced to bear the full brunt of my mother's substantial weight.

I felt a warm glow inside when Violet Burke observed that she could get used to the crisp freshness of the Greek evening air, free of the pervasive traffic pollution she was more accustomed to in Warrington.

"'Appen it's a benefit not having double deckers flying by, belching out mucky fumes. Mind you, a few lamp posts wouldn't go amiss. I'm of the age where my bones might be a bit too brittle for a night-time encounter with a pothole."

"I wouldn't worry, Vi. You've got plenty of padding," Barry teased.

"Aye, this Puffa's packed full of stuffing," she replied, ignoring Barry's intended meaning.

"Just remember to always carry a torch, Mother, to illuminate any hazards. Saying that, there are plenty of evenings when you can safely make your way through the village by moonlight since we don't suffer from light pollution over here."

"You don't have to keep trying to sell me on the place, lad. I'm already here," Vi pointed out.

"As if we couldn't fail to notice," Barry huffed under his breath as we finally reached our destination.

A clearly frazzled Doreen flung the door open. Rather than complaining that we were late, an involuntary scream escaped the mouth of our hostess as she confronted the balaclava topped bulbous form of Violet Burke on the doorstep, my mother's bulk obscuring the rest of us huddling behind her. Clearly rattled, Doreen raised her arms in the air as though being held up at gunpoint, before clapping her hands in front of her gaping mouth. A flash of yellow accompanied the sound of wet rubber slapping against skin: it appeared that we had caught Doreen up to her elbows in Marigolds.

"Get a grip," Violet Burke scoffed, ripping the balaclava off and pushing her way indoors.

"I didn't recognise you, Mrs Burke," Doreen said with a nervous laugh. "You scared the life out of me, pointing that thing at me with your face covered up."

"It's a bottle of cheap plonk, not a shotgun. Burglars would hardly be ringing the doorbell, you daft apeth," Vi pointed out.

"Sorry we're late." Even though I had no desire

to be there, my inherent good manners prompted me to apologise for our tardiness.

"You're the first to arrive, thank goodness. Norman's running behind and I haven't even had time to change yet," Doreen said, panic discernible in her voice as she self-consciously ran her hands over a drab nylon house-dress.

"'Cor, I had an overall just like that back in the 90s. It was right handy for keeping me grease free in the chippy," Violet Burke exclaimed.

Grappling with the buttons to remove the offending item, Doreen ushered Marigold, Barry and Violet Burke through to the living room. Grabbing my arm, she steered me into the kitchen. Peeling the Marigolds from her hands, she flapped them in front of my face, declaring, "Victor, I am counting on you to come to Norman's rescue before the whole evening descends into disaster."

The kitchen was nothing short of a chaotic shambles. Evidently when Norman attended my cookery classes, he had paid scant attention to the emphasis that I placed on cleaning up after oneself and maintaining a hygienically pristine environment. With his back turned, Norman hovered over a hotplate at the far end of the room, seemingly oblivious that it looked as though a bomb had gone off in the kitchen. With his attention focused on the hob, Norman chided his wife, "There's no need to exaggerate, Doreen. Everything is under control. The beef and olive stew is cooking away in the oven and I'm just seeing to the starter."

"I thought the idea behind one pot cooking was to cut down on the clutter," Doreen sighed, a defeated look in her eyes as her gaze lingered on the veritable mountain of dirty pots strewn on every surface and heaped high in the sink. Turning to me, she bewailed, "I told him that attempting a dessert of Charlotte Russe was too adventurous but you had to go and encourage him."

Clueless what Doreen was on about, I ignored her jibe. The penny dropped when she continued, "He'd never have tried it if you hadn't told him the Greek word for ladies' fingers. He couldn't make that old woman in the shop with the unpronounceable name understand that he wanted sponge fingers."

I made a mental note to avoid Norman's pudding course. When he had telephoned me earlier demanding to know the Greek word for ladies' fingers, I had presumed he was talking about okra and obligingly informed him to ask for *bamia*. It was a natural assumption since no self-respecting aspiring dessert chef would resort to cutting corners by using pre-packaged sponge fingers. I choked back an involuntary laugh at the thought of him attempting to line a fancy cake mould with the notoriously viscous vegetable. Surely even Norman couldn't be that dense.

"Damn and blast," Norman cried as something shot out of the pan he was tending, whizzing past my ear at the speed of a bullet before thwacking the kitchen cupboard behind my head.

"What on earth?" I uttered. Fingering the tip of my ear to check it was still attached, I was transfixed by the oily smear surrounding the sudden dent that appeared in the wood. My exclamation was drowned out in the barrage of scattershots erupting from Norman's pan. A series of violent mini explosions sent unidentified objects flying about the kitchen, forcing the three of us to duck.

"For goodness sake, take the pan off the heat," Doreen shrieked. There was a sickening crunch as my foot landed on one of the missiles that had exploded from the pan. Bending down to examine the mysterious object, I spotted something dark and pulpy surrounded by a greasy mess of trodden breadcrumbs. The crunching sound had presumably emanated from what appeared to be a now crushed pit. It dawned on me that Norman was attempting to prepare an appetiser of deep fried olives. It was no great surprise that it appeared to have gone hideously wrong.

"I told you it was a stupid idea to drop them into the chip pan," Doreen complained, a long suffering sneer evident in her tone.

"I didn't expect breaded olives to go off like popcorn," Norman protested. "I wonder if any of them are salvageable."

"Don't be ridiculous." Lowering her voice to a hiss, Doreen continued, "We can't very well serve olives scraped up from the floor with Victor watching. You know what a fuss pot he can be; he'd likely have an apoplectic fit."

Despite Doreen's attempts to be discreet, she had the type of voice that carried, ensuring that I overheard the comment most definitely not intended for my ears. I could only assume that if she hadn't dragged me into the kitchen, the pair of them would be down on the floor retrieving scattered olives and picking them clean of cat hairs and other assorted detritus before serving them up as an appetiser to their unsuspecting guests. Still, I was relieved that we wouldn't be expected to choke down olives that had experienced an unfortunate encounter with the flotsam floating around in the bottom of Doreen's chip pan.

"Well, at least we still have the stew to serve up," Norman said. "I followed your recipe to the tee, Victor. All I need to do is pop the olives in. I've been practising cooking up beef and olives every night to perfect it."

"Every single night," Doreen reiterated, emphasising her point with an exaggerated roll of her eyes. "I'm sick of the sight of it."

"Why didn't you try out one of the other dishes I've demonstrated in class?" I asked Norman, rather taken aback by his dedication to perfecting the recipe. "The *revithia* is simple to master."

"Was that the chickpea soup stuff? I was happy to give it a go but Doreen wasn't keen. Chickpeas play havoc with her wind."

"Victor doesn't want to hear about my digestive issues…" Doreen protested, her face turning puce.

"Your what? There's nothing unnatural about a bout of flatulence. You know how chestnuts set mine off but it doesn't stop me from enjoying them," Norman shared. It struck me that under the stress of preparing dinner, the usually reticent Norman had adopted the adage discretion be damned.

The sound of new arrivals interrupted their petty bickering. Doreen sent a pleading look in my direction before scurrying away to grant them admittance. I considered it a bit rich that after being dragged along unwillingly to attend an expat dinner party, the hostess had the cheek to expect me to slip my hands into the discarded Marigolds and restore the kitchen to order. I had no intention of obliging.

"Drat, I've deep fried every last olive and there's

none left to throw in the stew," Norman complained.

"You could try substituting the olives with capers," I suggested.

"Capers, right. Let's see if Doreen has a tin of the things," Norman said, frantically searching through the cupboards. "Won't it taste a bit odd if I mix fish with beef?"

"What have capers got to do with fish?" I queried.

"I thought they were...oh, never mind. Why don't you go through and join the others," Norman encouraged.

It sounded as though he was quite keen to get rid of me, making me a tad suspicious. I surmised he was eager for me to leave the kitchen so that he could start scrambling round on the floor, gathering up the exploded olives to throw in the casserole the moment the coast was clear.

"You could always serve it without the olives..." I began to say.

Doreen reappeared in the kitchen, figuratively clutching her pearls. There was a twinge of desperation in her voice as she demanded, "I need peanuts or crisps to pass round to our guests since you've messed up the appetiser."

"Is everyone here already?" Norman asked.

"Gordon and Moira just arrived. Can you

believe they've brought their dog along? I didn't invite it."

"What a blooming cheek," Norman agreed.

"It's not as though we take the cat along to dinner parties, it's hardly the done thing," Doreen moaned.

"Oh, I don't know. My gardener is off for a night on the town with his rabbit," I joshed.

"That's as maybe but you don't see your gardener being invited to select social gatherings," Doreen humphed, her dismissive opinion of Guzim clearly influenced by my wife.

A short, curly-haired creature bounded into the kitchen, transfixing our attention. Resembling a wind-up teddy bear in its cuteness, it made a beeline for the exploded olives littering the floor, snarfing them up as though they were a great delicacy. I watched with bemusement as what I presumed was the uninvited Waffles, the goldendoodle belonging to Gordon and Moira, polished off the missing ingredient in Norman's stew. I was relieved that we would be spared Norman sweeping them up and craftily chucking them in the pot.

"Hello, Victor. It's good to see you again. I can't wait to get to know Marigold," Moira said, narrowly avoiding an oily patch on the floor as she leant in to offer an air kiss before taking a firm hold of the dog's collar.

Moira and Gordon had only just returned to Greece after going back to England to collect their pet. Since they had left Meli before Marigold's return from England, the two women were yet to become acquainted. After completing the purchase of Leo's house, the Stranges decided to fly their dog over and spend the winter in Meli. I recalled Gordon telling me that his wife was keen to acclimatise the canine, though judging by its somewhat unnatural orange coat it looked as though it had already spent too long in the sun. Considering that Moira had been keen to learn of any pet grooming salons in the area, it was not beyond the realms of possibility that she had treated it to a tanning session under a sun lamp.

"Moira, I don't think your dog should be in the kitchen," Doreen carped. Not wishing to appear the ungracious hostess, she shifted the blame to me. "You know how Victor deplores anything unhygienic."

"Waffles is perfectly clean, I gave him a bath earlier," Moira trilled. "Goldendoodles hardly shed at all and are renowned for being super hypoallergenic..."

Moira paused mid-sentence, a gasp escaping her lips as Doreen's cat wandered into the kitchen, its hackles rising and tail bristling at the sight of the canine intruder. The feline's hiss attracted Waffles' attention and it romped over, playfully petting the cat. The dog's behaviour confirmed my suspicion that Moira had been bending the truth when she claimed the goldendoodle was terrified of cats: the look of panic transfusing her features indicated that she was the one with a pronounced case of ailuro-phobia, a condition Gordon had hinted at during our cave walk.

"I rather think that Moira is terrified of your cat," I discreetly whispered to Doreen.

"I'll put it out," she hissed back, belatedly re-membering to play the part of the good hostess. With the cat safely deposited outside, Doreen in-vited, "Moira, come through to the living room for a glass of wine and some nibbles. And do bring the dog; it shouldn't be in the kitchen."

"I must keep Waffles away from the crisps and peanuts. Too much salt gives him diarrhoea," Moira confided. It struck me that we were doomed to spend the evening discussing subjects all too closely related to the contents of Violet Burke's backed up toilet unless I could steer the conversa-tion towards more innocuous topics. With all this talk of flatulence and diarrhoea, I was beginning to see the attraction of tedious subjects like traffic cones and house prices.

Taking a last look at the bombsite kitchen, I ad-vised Doreen that Violet Burke may not be insulted if she offered to bung her a tenner to clean things up.

"But she's a guest." Doreen's blushing stammer indicated she had been browbeaten into including my mother amongst the numbers.

"So am I, supposedly." Relishing in the sarcasm, I cast a meaningful glance at the discarded Marigolds.

"Yes, but you're the one that got Norman into cooking," Doreen argued.

"At your behest," I reminded her. "I'm sure a messy kitchen is a small price to pay for keeping Norman from tippling his days away."

With that I retired to the living room to join the others, amused to see Doreen trotting after me and sidling up to my mother. I watched with interest as words were exchanged just beyond earshot, noting the way Violet Burke planted her feet firmly, making no move towards the kitchen. Clearly put in her place, Doreen resumed the rounds, topping up wine glasses and passing around some rather stale looking oregano crisps that Tina had been palming off at half-price: their best before date had expired at the end of the last century.

I was reluctant to impose myself on Marigold since she was deep in conversation with Moira, their tinkling laughter indicating they were getting on like a house on fire. The look on Doreen's face when the pair of them blithely waved away her offering of stale crisps was a picture, her nose demonstrably put out of joint by the instant rapport between the two women. In my opinion, Doreen relied rather too much on Marigold's company. I often suspected that my wife tended to tolerate the friendship: in all honesty, I couldn't envisage that Doreen and Norman would have been part of our social circle back in England but the dynamics of moving abroad tended to throw up the unlikeliest of friendships. It was hardly surprising. Although Marigold had formed excellent relationships with the Greek women of Meli, it was hard for her to establish deep bonds due to the challenge of communicating in a foreign language. The natural flow of chat was hindered by my wife's lack of fluency: conversation tended to centre on superficial topics such as sewing, cooking and gardening. It was easier for me since the male friendships I had forged didn't revolve around the more deep and meaningful aspects of life that women habitually bond over. I was happy to spend an evening in the company of the non-English speaking Panos, passing the time talking about nothing more taxing than chickens and vegetables.

Deciding to take pity on Doreen, I accepted a crisp, planning to feed it to the goldendoodle once her back was turned. "Has everyone arrived or are you expecting anyone else?" I asked.

"Edna and Milton are late but once they arrive we can sit down and eat." Lowering her voice to a whisper, Doreen continued, "I was in two minds over whether or not to invite Sherry but thought better of it after I heard how she tried to seduce you when Marigold was in England."

"That was just a silly misunderstanding," I assured her. "Marigold would hate for you to exclude Sherry over that."

"Yes, but Barry would have been an odd number for Sherry to latch onto and I didn't think Marigold would approve of that."

Doreen's reply explained why my mother had been roped in to make up the numbers at short notice. Doreen was a stickler for not having odd numbers at her table even if some of the guests she included were distinctly odd by nature. I stifled a snort at the thought that strange may be a more apt word than odd now that the Stranges had been embraced by the expat dining club. Not that there was anything strange about them of course.

"I was rather under the impression that Sherry was walking out with Dimitris," I said.

"Walking out with. You do have a funny way of putting things, Victor. I haven't heard that old chestnut for years," Doreen laughed.

"So are they an item or not?" I demanded a tad

too brusquely, my natural curiosity getting the better of me even if it did make me look as though I was a convert to Marigold's endless matchmaking. In truth, I was keen to see Sherry paired off: one never knew when she might get desperate enough to turn her fancy towards me again if no one more available came along for her to latch her claws into.

"I don't know. They don't look very lovey-dovey during your cookery classes."

"Well, my classes are hardly the time nor the place for canoodling. There are sharp knives involved," I pointed out.

"That Sherry has been throwing her money around on some fella," Violet Burke volunteered, sidling up next to me and dipping her hands into the bowl of crisps.

"Really," Doreen simpered, her voice tremulous with the prospect of some juicy gossip.

"Bit of a scruff, I'd say, he could certainly do with a haircut. Course Sherry is that desperate to land a fella that she can't see he's just using her for her money; she's practically furnishing his house for him."

Whilst Dimitris was certainly in desperate need of a decent haircut, he had never struck me as the materialistic type nor the type to take advantage of a woman. Before Doreen or I could press my mother to elaborate and confirm our suspicions that

Sherry was lavishing cash on Dimitris, Violet Burke said, "I stuck my head round the kitchen door. I can give it a going over first thing in the morning but it will take more than a tenner, it's like a pigsty in there."

"Okay, fifteen then," Doreen agreed. "Have another crisp, Victor, in fact take the bowl. I really must see how Norman is getting on in the kitchen."

"You should have held out for twenty," I advised my mother, surreptitiously feeding stale oregano crisps to the grateful Waffles. "There's a good chance you may end up having to mop up dog diarrhoea."

Chapter 8

A Canine Foot Warmer

I say, something prowling around outside the house set the cats off, what. It was all I could do to drag Edna away from them, she hates to see them agitated," Milton announced when the Hancocks finally deigned to show up. Claiming a spot close to the fire, Milton rubbed his frozen hands together, causing the wine to slop over the edge of his glass. I noticed he looked a tad under the weather, liver spots standing out in stark relief against the white, papery skin of his hands.

"Let's hope that Panos' ferocious guard dog hasn't escaped its chain again," Marigold shuddered, disturbed by the idea of something unknown on the prowl.

"Dogs are a menace to cats, what…" Milton declared, instantly changing his tune when Waffles moseyed over, rubbing its curly coat against his leg. "Oh, I say, old chap, where did you spring from?"

Despite opining that dogs were a menace, Milton seemed quite taken with the attractive creature.

"I do hope Waffles isn't bothering you. He's quite harmless," Gordon said.

"Some kind of hybrid mutt, is it, what? Handsome fellow," Milton observed, shamelessly encouraging Waffles to lick the sticky wine from his fingers.

"He's a goldendoodle." Gordon's indulgent tone made him sound like a proud parent.

"A what?"

"It's a cross between a Labrador and a poodle," Gordon explained. "Fortunately he doesn't have the yapping nature of a poodle, in fact he rarely barks at all."

"It's not much use as a guard dog without a bark," I observed.

"Waffles is a he, not an it," Moira corrected, sticking limpet-like to Marigold as my wife edged closer to the fire. "And goldendoodles are a designer breed."

"Ah, designer. Got you," Milton piped up.

"Edna's convinced that some of our adopted strays have a touch of pedigree cat in them…"

"I very much doubt it," Marigold interjected. "My cats are the only pedigrees in the village and they certainly aren't in the habit of slipping out to the bins to engage in promiscuous behaviour."

Marigold had a point. It was rare for her precious imported domestics, the overly coddled Clawsome and Catastrophe, to leave the house or mix with other cats. I hoped she wasn't going to voice her opinion that Edna should have her strays seen to by a veterinarian: such a contentious subject would invariably lead to squabbling over the dinner table. Whilst I shared her opinion that the village was so overrun with ferals that one could barely make it down the street without tripping over a random cat, the Hancocks barely had the funds to feed their adopted clowder, let alone fork out for luxuries such as neutering and spaying.

Announcing that dinner was served, Doreen rushed everyone to the outside terrace where a table was laid for ten. Along with my fellow guests, I was clearly bewildered that Doreen expected us to leave the warmth of the blazing log fire to dine alfresco, the evening temperature hardly conducive to such folly without the risk of us all succumbing to a nasty bout of pneumonia. Hastily throwing a bulky sweater over her frock, Doreen gestured towards a set of clear plastic blinds suspended from the wooden awning. Rigged up in an amateur fashion to enclose the dining table from the elements, they flapped nosily in the wind.

"Norman fitted these blinds so it would be nice and warm to eat outside..." The intrusive rustle of thrashing plastic practically drowned out Doreen's voice. The howling draught blasting in beneath the blinds made me wish that I had taken the precaution of adding an extra pair of socks. Fortunately, a bit of quick thinking meant I was able to lure Waffles over as a foot warmer, the goldendoodle proving a sucker for a cheap bribe of stale crisps. Hopefully, the dog would be as amenable to hoovering up Norman's stew if it turned out to be as inedible as I anticipated.

I watched in amusement as Marigold, with a deft sleight of hand, switched the place cards to position herself next to Moira. My amusement was short lived when I realised that Marigold's messing with the name tags left me seated next to Norman. Since our host had as much charisma as a bowl of congealed porridge, I substituted his place card for Barry's as soon as Doreen headed off to the kitchen.

Peering intently over the rim of the rectangular glasses perched on the edge of her nose, Violet Burke grabbed the seat opposite Barry, flicking Milton's place card to the other end of the table.

Muttering under her breath, she explained, "I can do without that Milton fella trying to play footsie with me under the table."

Nudging me sharply in the ribs, Barry hissed, "When did Edna transform from a harmless looking pensioner into a painted woman?"

I gawped in disbelief as Edna took the seat opposite me. She appeared to have undergone a bizarre makeover that left her resembling a startled porcelain doll. Her new look screamed of desperation, smeared blue eye shadow running into trowelled on blusher. I assumed that determined to outshine the perceived competition of Violet Burke, Edna had spent an age shovelling the slap on, using an actual shovel by the looks of it.

"You've got to feel sorry for her," Barry whispered in my ear. "It looks as though she's trying to recreate herself as Brandy."

"Brandy?"

"That tart in Milton's mucky book…"

"Don't tell me you've been reading his porn."

"I had a sneaky look at Cynthia's signed copy. It's dreadful drivel."

"I hope my mother isn't going to put her foot in it," I said, cringing inwardly as Violet Burke leant in to speak to Edna. The contrast between the two pensioners was marked: my mother, renowned for coating her face in too much slap, had on this occasion made no effort at all appearance wise beyond running her hands through her balaclava messed hair.

"Here, your eye shadow has missed your lid." Peering at Edna, my mother spat on a voluminous handkerchief retrieved from the sleeve of her cardie before aiming the soggy cloth in the direction of the other woman's face.

"I just wanted to make a bit of an effort but I can't make out what I'm doing with these cataracts," Edna admitted.

"You need to get yourself one of them magnifying mirrors. I know that Sherry swears by hers, she says she'd never be able to pluck the hairs out of her chin without one."

"You'll be out of a cleaning job if you go around spreading confidences about your employers," I warned my mother as she busied herself wiping the gunk off Edna's face.

"I speak as I find. If my employers want to keep their business private then they should have the common sense to lock anything incriminating away before I start scrubbing," my mother said sagely. I made a mental note to stash Harold's surplus supply of Grecian 2000 in a locked cabinet before Violet Burke next got to grips with our bathroom. Just because we were related, there was no guarantee that my mother wouldn't blab to all and sundry about what I got up to with a bottle of lotion within the privacy of my bathroom.

Returning from the kitchen, Doreen's eyes narrowed in annoyance when she clocked all the men lined up on one side of the table, facing the women on the other. Her careful seating plan had been thrown into complete disarray, her strict line-up of boy-girl gone with the wind. My analogy was quite apt since Marigold wasted no time excusing the re-arranged seating plan by blatantly fibbing, telling Doreen, "That shocking draught blowing in sent the place cards flying all over the place."

Sandwiched between Gordon and Barry, I was relieved to be out of spitting distance of Norman. "I've done that Greek beef and olive stew from Victor's classes," our host announced, neglecting to mention the stew was devoid of olives.

"Stew, eh, just the ticket for dining outside in the cold." Milton's breath was visibly suspended in the frigid air as he exhaled.

"So, tell me how did this expat dinner club get off the ground?" Moira asked with genuine interest whilst the rest of us shivered. I assumed that Moira and Gordon didn't appear to feel the cold since they had not been in Greece long enough to acclimatise: perchance to them, Doreen's plastic wrapped draughty terrace was warm in comparison to the temperatures the couple were accustomed to back in England.

"It was Doreen's brainchild. It gives us a chance to get together and sample different cuisines from around the globe," Marigold said.

"Yes, the idea is that we cook up a meal from foreign parts for each gathering," Doreen added.

"Does Greek food technically count as foreign fare since we're in Greece?" Moira pressed.

"Can't say it does, old girl. Thought the old rules stated we have to serve up grub from foreign countries. I remember how Edna pulled out all the stops and did Kenyan," Milton said.

Recalling the Hancocks attempt to go foreign, I cringed. Drawing inspiration from their days in Kenya, Edna had served up some slop she swore was authentic African irio, a dish of boiled and mashed corn, potatoes and peas. When I later plugged the name of the insubstantial dish of mush into Google, it revealed that irio was a side dish intended to be served with grilled steak. Clearly the impoverished Hancocks had cut corners by depriving us of the steak and doing their dinner on the cheap. Even their adopted strays had turned their collective noses up at such slop.

"I experimented with some French dishes..." Doreen said.

"And Victor's curries are very popular. Will you be teaching us how to do Greek curry in your classes?" Norman asked.

"There's no such thing as Greek curry," I enlightened him.

"Ah, right, that would explain why we can't get one down on the coast," Norman said. "Always thought it was odd, so many restaurants but not one of them doing an Indian."

"Well it strikes me that doing Greek food for the foreign dinner parties is cheating, what," Milton opined. I considered Milton should keep his opinions to himself since he was always eager enough to take the leftovers home whenever he had the good fortune to be invited out to dinner.

"I could barely manage beans on toast before Victor's classes. I thought I would serve up one of his recipes to show my progress in the kitchen." Norman hovered over the casserole dish beaming as proudly as though he was just about to plate up his first new-born. As he slopped the stew onto plates, I intercepted a withering look from my wife. "Victor, tell me you aren't feeding those crisps to the dog."

"Wouldn't dream of it," I lied, patting my furry companion beneath the table.

"Poor Waffles was so traumatised by the plane ride over that we may have to rethink our plans," Gordon said.

"How so?" I asked.

"Well, Moira doesn't want to put Waffles through the torment of flying backwards and forwards to England after his terrible ordeal in the hold," Gordon elaborated.

"I think it was the separation he found most traumatic. He's been terribly clingy ever since he put his paws back on land," Moira added.

"So, we've decided we may have to make Meli our main base and take it in turns to fly back home when work dictates. That way, one of us would always be here for Waffles," Gordon continued.

"And it would spare him the separation anxiety he endured flying as cargo." The way Moira fussed, anyone would think that the dog had been professionally analysed by a shrink.

"You could always drive the dog back, old girl," Milton suggested.

"It's a long trip by road and Waffles might get sick on the ferry. He's got a very sensitive stomach," Moira revealed.

"It's no picnic transporting animals by car either. We brought our cats over by road and ferry. I wouldn't put my precious darlings through that journey again," Marigold sympathised.

"Oh, poor things. Were they sick?" Moira asked solicitously, hiding her loathing of cats from her new cat-loving best friend.

"Not as sick as Barry," I said.

"You could always try dosing up your dog with the local remedy of vinegar and honey, I found it worked wonders," Barry suggested.

"I wouldn't risk it. Honey can lead to diarrhoea if it's fed to dogs with sensitive stomachs." It struck me that Moira was a tad obsessive when it came to Waffle's digestive system. The crisps she had warned me against feeding the pampered golden-doodle didn't appear to have done it any harm: it was snoozing away comfortably on my feet.

Perhaps twigging that the dog's digestive system was a tad off-putting as a topic of conversation for the dinner table, Gordon hastily changed the subject. "Moira wants to make some changes to the house…"

"We'd only originally intended it to be a holiday home but if we are staying any length of time we'll have to refurnish," Moira interrupted.

"Thought that house you bought was all done up with mod cons, what," Milton said.

"Oh, yes, it's done to a high standard but the furnishings that came with it aren't to my taste," Moira said.

"Well, the chap that was in there before you was getting on, what," Milton said, seemingly oblivious that Leo had been younger than him.

"I want to put my own stamp on it but I'm clueless about the best places to shop over here."

"Marigold's your woman, got a fine reputation for interior décor," Milton volunteered. "Heard she did marvellous things with that Albanian chap's home. Very inventive."

"And pink," I muttered.

"Really, that would be super. Perhaps I could see his house for inspiration, Marigold," Moira suggested.

"Guzim's a bit shy about showing off his shed," I jumped in, imagining my Albanian gardener squirming at the thought of the pink palace of love being thrown open for public display again.

"And I doubt he's maintained it in the showroom condition I left it in," Marigold added. "I'd be happy to give you a tour of the furniture shops in town, Moira."

"That would be wonderful. We could make a day of it," Moira trilled, beaming with pleasure as Marigold flattered her by saying how lovely her ears were and how satisfying it must be to model them for a living. "So, Marigold, were you an interior decorator back in England?"

"No, I was in food standards…"

Before Marigold could complete her sentence, Violet Burke cackled, "Was she heck as like. Marigold was a pet food taster, have you ever heard the like?"

Bristling with indignation at my mother's

mocking tone, Marigold retorted, "It is a serious profession, Vi. It requires a degree in food science."

"I've told you before, Mother, one can't just walk in off the street and land a job by professing one's love for chowing down on a tin of Pedigree Chum," I said in my wife's defence. "Marigold's job was vital in ensuring domestic pets received a diet of safe, tasty and nutritious food prepared in hygienic surroundings."

"I never realised that pet food tasters were an actual thing. Now that I think of it, I can see what an important role they fulfil," Moira gushed.

"Must be difficult to force yourself to get pet food down, what," Milton interrupted. "I remember the times we had nothing but tinned cat food in the house but I couldn't bring myself to eat it. Rather go to bed hungry, what."

"There were certainly times when we were tempted and tried to convince ourselves that if we spread it on toast it would be just like eating *paté.* In the end we just couldn't bring ourselves to do it, we couldn't bear to deprive the cats," Edna reminded him.

"That frumpy friend of Marigold's, what's her name, Geraldine? She's another pet food taster. Got herself addicted to bird seed and piled on the pounds…" Violet Burke interjected.

"Geraldine is not frumpy…" Marigold pointlessly protested.

"I'd never have thought of bird seed as fattening, I mean you don't see many fat birds," Barry said.

"Not unless they're old slappers," Milton guffawed.

"Have you been hanging round in the Dirty Bird again, Milton?" Violet Burke sarcastically enquired. Her reference to the Pelican Pub where Milton had first become entranced by his dream woman did not escape Edna's notice.

"Milton does not frequent public houses," Edna declared snootily.

"Difficult for overweight birds to get airborne, I should imagine," Gordon observed, his innocuous remark dispelling the tension brewing between Edna and Vi.

"Can't beat a bit of suet for feeding the birds," Vi said. "Speaking of suet, this stew wouldn't half taste better with a generous serving of dumplings."

"Dumplings don't sound very Greek," Gordon said.

"Well, they must exist as there's a Greek word for them. I saw it in the dictionary," Marigold volunteered, not bothering to elaborate despite everyone staring at her expectantly, no doubt keen to add this vital winter word to their limited Greek vocabulary. "I don't know what it is; I only know that there is one."

"*Zymarika*," I dutifully obliged.

"Come again, old chap." My translation had clearly confused Milton.

"The Greek word for dumplings is *zymarika*," I repeated.

"There's no point in knowing the word for dumplings when they don't sell suet over here. It's a peculiar place that doesn't have dumplings in winter. If I'd known it would be impossible to come by, I'd have brought some over in my suitcase," Violet Burke grumbled.

"You might have had difficulty squeezing it in alongside your chip pan and hot water bottle," Marigold scoffed, still clearly annoyed that my mother had spurned her thoughtful gifts of a spanking new deep fat fryer and electric blanket. I hoped that my wife didn't discover that Violet Burke had palmed the brand new fryer off on the Jehovah's Witness; it would be like rubbing salt in the wound.

As my mother chuntered on about suet, I unsuccessfully suppressed a snort, recalling how she had amused herself by teaching Vasos that the English word for cushion was suet dumpling.

"What's that smirk for, lad?"

"Just thinking about Captain Vasos and dumplings..."

"Captain Vasos?" Moira raised one eyebrow in

query.

"He's a friend of mine, got a yacht he has," Violet Burke jumped in.

"It's a pleasure boat," I clarified.

"If I was twenty years younger, I'd be giving serious consideration to his mucky suggestions." A vulgar wink accompanied Violet Burke's words.

"Doesn't sound like a gentleman, what." Colour flooded Milton's pale cheeks; amazingly he reddened rather than turning green.

"Really, Vi, must you be so crude?" Marigold chided.

"We had a grand night out with Vasos when you were gadding about in Manchester, didn't we Victor?"

"Marigold wasn't gadding," I snapped. My recollection of the evening in question remained somewhat vague: the last thing I wanted was my mother bandying the sordid details over the dinner table.

"Next time I go back to England, Violet, I'll bring you some suet," Gordon offered. "This stew is excellent, Norman, really tasty."

"Can't find any olives in mine," Milton complained.

"Waffles' stomach is so delicate, just the hint of salt goes right through his digestive tract," Moira volunteered, returning to her pet subject. "Perhaps you could give me some insider tips on his dietary requirements, Marigold."

As Moira spoke, I detected an ominous rumble emanating from under the table where Waffles was curled up sleeping on my feet. I experienced a twinge of guilt for feeding the dog stale salty crisps.

"I would recommend sticking to tried and tested popular brands rather than cutting corners with the cheap stuff," Marigold advised. "And be careful about anything the dog snacks on."

"He ate those olives off Doreen's kitchen floor earlier," Moira said in a worried tone as the rumblings from under the table grew ever louder.

"Oh, that's not good," Marigold cautioned. "Olives that have fallen off the trees outside are fine but you need to be careful about dogs eating cured olives. Too much salt and oil…"

I tuned out, snippets of conversation about traffic cones, house prices and dogs' dietary needs drifting around the periphery of my conscience. Almost numb from cold, I imagined warming my hands in front of Nikos' welcoming *somba* in the taverna, the challenge of mentally translating the chatter of Greek locals sure to keep me engaged even if the subjects of conversation were as dull as those at Doreen's table.

Barry nudged me sharply in the ribs. Turning to my brother-in-law, I wished that the two of us could escape the tedium and take refuge in the privacy of his frog-infested shed.

"What?"

"Norman is trying to get your attention," Barry replied.

"What do you think of the *vodino katsaroles me elies?*" Norman practically bellowed at me from across the table, the Greek words clearly laboured though obviously well-rehearsed in anticipation of this moment. Everyone swivelled their heads to focus on me, eager to see how the teacher would rate his student's performance. Realising that I had barely touched the congealed mess of now tepid beef on my plate, I made an enthusiastic stab at it with my fork.

"Technically you should rename the dish *vodino katsaroles horis elies,*" I said, popping a morsel of food into my mouth and forcing a look of fake pleasure on my face as I chewed. It wouldn't be good for business if the recipes I taught in my classes turned into culinary flops when my students' put them into practice. Masticating the leathery beef, I hoped that the expression I conveyed was one of appreciation rather than contorted gurning.

"What's that when it's at home?" Norman asked.

"Beef stew without olives," I replied, wondering how I could distract attention away from myself and feed the rest of my stew to the sleeping dog.

Chapter 9

The Wanderer Returns

Well, eat up. I've done a Charlotte Russe for pudding," Norman instructed, pointedly refusing the wine Barry offered and sticking to water.

"We may have to skip dessert," Marigold said apologetically.

"Oh, no, there's no skipping out on my pudding. I've been practising my patisserie skills for the last fortnight. I rather think afters are my forte, I seem to have a natural bent."

I was surprised to hear Norman speak with such confidence. He had a tendency to be a tad wishy-washy unless he was pontificating about his specialist subject of traffic cones. It seemed that Doreen had been spot on when she credited my cookery classes with injecting some get-up-and-go into his jaded life.

"But it is your first attempt at Charlotte Russe," Doreen reminded her husband, apparently a tad apprehensive how it may turn out. "It's a bit trickier to master than those éclairs you did. I must have put on half a stone taste testing Norman's éclairs, they were positively Moorish."

Instead of leaping to his wife's defence and doing his husbandly duty by proclaiming Doreen hadn't put on any weight, Norman instead urged, "It really would be helpful, Victor, if you added desserts to your cookery classes."

"He's got a yen to master exotic confections," Doreen said.

"Like what?" Barry asked.

"I've been browsing the cook books and fancy having a go at profiteroles and mille-feuilles. Then there's Macarons and Madeleines though they look a bit tricky."

"I don't see why you want to bother," Barry said. "You can just order a box of Mr Kipling's fondant fancies from the British Corner Shop."

"Is that a shop in town?" Violet Burke asked. "'Appen they'd have some suet and some proper brown sauce."

"It's an online store, Mother. They deliver British food to Greece but the postage is terribly pricey."

"I have to say, Norman, your list sounds a bit ambitious for an amateur," Marigold advised. "It would be much easier to get to grips with a nice lemon drizzle to start with."

Ignoring Marigold's opinion, Norman continued, "And with Christmas looming, I was thinking of a rich fruit cake with marzipan and icing, and a stollen."

"Lidl do a lovely stollen," Marigold pointed out.

"What do you think, Victor? Do you fancy including fancy desserts in your classes?" Norman persisted.

"My classes focus on Greek dishes, Norman. I'd be happy to include *bougatsa* and *baklava*," I offered, inwardly cursing when I realised it would involve brushing up on my inept pastry skills. To say my feeble attempts to get to grips with pastry lacked professionalism was an understatement.

"What's wrong with a proper British pudding?" Violet Burke piped up. "You can pop round to mine, lad. I'll give you a crash course in turning out a nice treacle tart and a jam roly-poly. Or 'appen you'd rather get started with spotted dick or a moist pineapple upside down cake."

"Have you tried getting hold of a pineapple in Greece, Vi?" Barry chortled.

"I'm sure the Greeks have heard of tins," Vi retorted.

"Anyway, as I was saying, we may have to skip dessert," Marigold reiterated.

"You don't need to worry about Norman's pudding piling pounds on your waistline, Marigold. You've such a lovely figure," Doreen flattered. I guessed she was taking the sycophantic approach because she was feeling threatened by the budding friendship developing between Marigold and Moira.

"Oh, it's not that, you know I have a sweet tooth," Marigold assured her. "We left some unexpected visitors at home. They arrived quite out of the blue. We weren't expecting them until next week."

"Speak for yourself, I wasn't expecting them at all," I muttered under my breath.

"You didn't say. You could have brought them along..." Doreen's words dripped with insincerity.

"What was that you were saying about visitors? 'Appen I'll pop up in the morning and say hello," Violet Burke declared.

"You're doing Doreen's kitchen first thing in the morning," I reminded my mother, making a mental note to have a quiet word with her at the first opportunity. It would be prudent to warn Violet Burke that our visitors had seen her pestering Gary, acting like a deranged old harridan as she harangued him about being his mother. It wouldn't do for her to be recognised: she would hate for the shameful truth about her abandoning me in a bucket to come out and become public knowledge in Meli. Not to mention, of course, that I would never live it down.

"Turned up out of the blue, you say. Awkward, what. We had a strange chap land on our doorstep when we first moved to Meli, never did have a clue who he was even though he stayed for a week," Milton said. With all the attention focused on Milton, I poked Waffles. As the dog reluctantly woke from his slumber, I sneaked it the rest of my stew. "Do you remember him, Edna?"

"He said he'd run into you when you were on that assignment in Kampala…but you never could place him," Edna replied.

"I remember how he gave you the willies…"

Edna crinkled her nose in disdain. "Well, he seemed to be a bit too intimately acquainted with Idi Amin for my liking."

"Think the old chap just liked to name drop, what…"

"Idi Amin is hardly the type usually favoured

by name droppers," I pointed out.

"I didn't trust him and the cats didn't take to him at all," Edna elaborated.

"Ah, yes, I remember," Milton said, punctuating his words with emphatic nods. "He got right up your nose when he kept boasting about shooting big cats."

"I don't think it was all talk, that leopard skin jerkin he wore still had the ears attached." I hazarded a guess that Edna's visible shiver was down to the memory of their sinister sounding visitor rather than the cold. Addressing the table, Edna confided, "I did try to warn Milton about him but he sees the best in everyone. He made off with Milton's Kenyan coin collection…"

"They'd have been worth a few bob by now," Milton lamented.

"Well, I'm sure we've nothing to worry about with our visitors," Marigold said, her brow beginning to furrow with worry. "Bill is big in the neighbourhood watch."

"According to him. We don't really know a thing about him," I said.

"We never have any overseas visitors to worry about," Doreen said morosely. "I blame Norman's traffic cones."

The mention of traffic cones prompted me to say, "Probably best if we make a move quite soon."

BUCKET TO GREECE (VOL.10)

"After Norman's Charlotte Russe," Marigold argued, having changed her tune at the prospect of sampling the classic French cake. She remained oblivious that the budding patisserie chef may have moronically substituted sponge fingers with okra.

"It wouldn't hurt you to miss your pudding for once…"

My words were drowned out by the unmistakable trumping sound of Waffles giving vent to a nasty dose of flatulence. Since the dog was still surreptitiously positioned on my feet under the table, it must have appeared to the room at large that I was responsible for the emission of foul-smelling flatus.

Springing to my feet, I lunged at Doreen's plastic blinds, wafting them around in a desperate attempt to let some fresh air in and disperse the sulphurous odour of rotten eggs tinged with oregano. "It's not me, it's the dog."

Judging from the looks of sheer incredulity that greeted my words as my fellow diners pinched their noses and hastily backed away from the table in disgust, my denial wasn't very convincing. Determined to absolve myself of blame for creating such a noxious odour, I confessed, "Perhaps I shouldn't have fed all those stale crisps to Waffles."

"It's not as bad as the stink from my backed up toilet," Violet Burke declared. Remaining a solitary figure at the table, she appeared oblivious to the pervasive pong, continuing to shovel stew into her mouth.

"I hardly think that the contents of your toilet are a suitable conversation for the dinner table," Milton grumbled. His words took me by surprise: it was the first time I had ever heard him say anything remotely negative to my mother. Edna's self-satisfied smirk hinted that her husband's curt tone had won him brownie points with his wife.

Frantically flapping the blinds, I noticed Waffles forcing itself to an upright position before lumbering out from under the table. Groaning piteously, it let rip with another vile smelling fart.

"How can anything so cute produce such a disgusting smell?" Marigold cried.

"You're just biased because you're married to him," Norman said, apparently still clueless that the dog, rather than me, was responsible for the disgusting stench.

"My son is passably handsome but I'd never describe him as cute," Violet Burke snorted.

"Not Victor, the dog," Marigold shouted in exasperation. "Do you seriously believe I would have married a man who would be crass enough to pass wind in the middle of a dinner party?"

"Well I married Doreen and she has a terrible issue with gas," Norman said.

BUCKET TO GREECE (VOL.10)

Firing daggers at her husband, Doreen shouted, "I refuse to have a flatulent dog at my dinner table."

"I told you it wasn't me," I said smugly.

"You should never have brought the dog along when it isn't house-trained," Doreen snapped at Moira.

"Waffles *is* house-trained. He just has a delicate stomach," Moira protested.

"Well it will have to go in the garden. Norman, put the dog in the garden at once," Doreen instructed. Grabbing a can of air freshener, she shook it vigorously before spraying with gay abandon until all her guests succumbed to violent fits of coughing. Despite her best efforts, the artificial scent did nothing to mask the pungent smell the dog had unleashed, the plastic blinds effectively trapping it in the enclosed outdoor space.

"Perhaps we should adjourn to the living room for dessert," Norman proposed. His suggestion was met with a positive stampede as everyone made a mad dash to get out of the cold and claim first dibs on a warm spot near the log fire, well away from the lingering funky smell.

When Milton cornered Marigold by the fire, she sent a pleading look in my direction, willing me to rescue her. My wife had little time for our elderly neighbour, preferring to palm him off with surplus lemon drizzle rather than actually engage in conversation. I put it down to her loathing of being addressed as 'old girl.'

Unfortunately, Milton was in full spiel before I had the opportunity to steer Marigold clear of his company.

"Haven't seen you since you got back from England, old girl. Hope everything was tickety-boo, what," Milton said. "Where was it you got to again?"

"Manchester…"

"Funny place to go for a holiday."

"I was staying with my friend, Geraldine. You may have run into her when she visited us here in Meli…"

"Ah, I know the one. Spotted her canoodling with that bearded chap that wears a long dress, what…"

"That's not a dress, it's his clerical vestment," I pointed out.

"Can't say I twigged he was religious." Scrunching his forehead, Milton stared at the ceiling as though waiting for divine confirmation about Andreas' calling.

Staring at Milton as though he had lost the plot, Marigold said incredulously, "But you were there when he conducted the traditional house blessing ceremony not long after we moved in."

"Ah, wondered why he was wafting the basil

around…takes all sorts. Can't say I ever ventured up north after the war, what. Has it changed much, old girl?"

"Since the war?" Marigold asked.

"No, since you up-sticked and came over here."

Fortunately Marigold was spared from answering when smoke started billowing out from the fire. Losing his train of thought, Milton switched topics.

"Looks like Harold is burning new wood," Milton said.

"Harold? Are you losing your marbles, Milton? Our host is Norman. Harold was that dreadful oik with the swimming pool."

"Quite. I'd better go and have a word with the old chap, what. Ought to be chucking aged logs on the fire or he'll bung up his chimney with tar." It occurred to me that Milton's routine manner of addressing everyone as old chap may be a deliberate ploy to disguise creeping dementia: I had always assumed it was a pretentious habit he'd picked up in Africa, but on the other hand he may just be bad with names.

As Milton wandered off, Marigold hissed in my ear excitedly, "I have it on good authority that Sherry has hooked herself a man…"

"I suppose that you have been listening to my mother," I hissed back. Whilst it would be an immense relief to know that another man had indeed gazumped me in Sherry's fickle affections, I didn't place much credence in any gossip originating from Violet Burke.

"She is in and out of Sherry's all the time with her cleaning job," Marigold pointed out. "Apparently Sherry is squandering her money on some man but your mother doesn't know who he is."

"She did mention something about a scruffy fellow with long hair..." I posited.

"Dimitris?" Marigold suggested.

I replied with a shrug. Dimitris could hardly be described as a scruff: he invariably wore a tie and kept his long thinning locks tied back in a ponytail.

"Well, I can't understand why she's keeping whoever it is under wraps. I had coffee with her yesterday and she never mentioned she had a new man in her life..."

As Marigold speculated about Sherry's love life, I spotted Gordon and Moira casting worried looks through the window, constantly checking on the welfare of their over-indulged pet, now safely installed in the garden. With the dog excommunicated from polite company, I keenly felt the loss. Since the canine dustbin appeared to be lacking any taste buds, I had anticipated it would eagerly wolf down my no doubt inedible experimental Charlotte Russe.

No sooner had I mentally conjured the dessert

than Doreen presented me with a plate heaped high with the fancy Victorian cake. I cautiously prodded it with my dessert fork, fully expecting to find a layer of green okra lurking beneath the whipped cream. To my surprise, my fork encountered nothing more ominous than a perfectly normal looking layer of sponge.

"I hadn't realised Norman was making a cake when he telephoned to ask me the Greek word for ladies' fingers. I thought he was talking about okra when I told him to ask for *bamia*," I confided to Doreen.

"I did think that you'd been playing a practical joke on him when he came home with okra."

"If I'd known he was baking, I would have told him to ask for *pantespani*."

"*Pantespani*. What's that?"

"Sponge cake."

"Well, knowing Norman, he'd have mixed up the pronunciation and come home with a pair of Y-fronts. He can't get that old woman in the shop to understand a word that he says. I'm sure she does it on purpose," Doreen said, as though Kyria Kompogiannopoulou's inability to communicate in English was a deliberate ploy to inconvenience them.

"The service was much better when you were behind the counter," Doreen added with a bemused smile. "Not to worry about the mix up, I fed the okra to the cat. It's not fussy like those pampered creatures of yours."

Taking the plunge, I forked a smidgen of Charlotte Russe into my mouth. Savouring the contrast between the tangy mousse and the rich cream, I was unable to conceal my genuine shock that Norman's confection was not only edible but positively scrumptious. "I say, this cake is delicious."

"Amazing isn't it? I never knew Norman had it in him. It's almost worth all that mess in the kitchen."

"Not to worry, my mother will have it sparkling in the morning."

"If Norman keeps on turning out desserts as good as this, I will soon be the size of a house," Doreen quipped.

"You'll have to join Marigold on one of her walks. Great way to keep trim," I suggested.

"If she's still got time for me," Doreen muttered, casting a jealous glance over to where Marigold and Moira were giggling together.

The room descended into silence as everyone discovered the wonders of Norman's masterful Charlotte Russe and tucked in with appreciation. It appeared I wasn't the only one to have underestimated Norman's burgeoning talent in the patisserie department. The gentle tinkle of dessert forks against china was suddenly drowned out by a thud emanating from the garden, followed by a series of timid yowls.

"Oh dear, it sounds as though Guzim has taken a short cut through your garden…he's terribly clumsy," Marigold said.

"Guzim?" Gordon queried.

"The Albanian who lives in the shed," I reminded him. "You ran into him on the night that fox created havoc in my chicken coop."

Gordon pressed his nose against the window, jumping backwards when a cacophony of guttural meowing and hissing erupted, piercing our eardrums.

"Oh, my goodness," Moira cried in alarm. "It sounds as though a gang of cats is terrorising Waffles. Do something, Gordon."

With Gordon hot-footing it out to the garden, Barry grabbed my arm. "We'd better go with him. Whatever it is sounds more like a maniac than a cat."

Reluctantly joining them in the drizzle, I struggled to discern anything in the dark. As Gordon called out to the dog, it hurled itself at its owner: whimpering plaintively, it almost bowled him over. A flash of flying fur caught my attention: in the blink of an eye whatever it was landed on Waffles' back, hissing like a thing possessed as it attacked the dog. Grabbing the torch from my pocket, I directed the beam towards Waffles.

"I don't believe it…I just don't believe it…"

"What?" Barry asked. "I can't make out a thing."

"Cynthia's vile cat is tearing into the dog. You did say whatever it was sounded like a maniac."

"Kouneli? Are you sure?"

"I thought for sure we'd seen the back of it but I'd recognise that mutant tom anywhere. Grab hold of it, Barry, before it does some damage to the dog."

Grasping the cat by the scruff of its neck, Barry held it up at arm's length to examine it. Whooping with delight, he pronounced, "You're right, the cat has come back. Cynthia will be over the moon."

"She'll have some grovelling to do to my mother. Cynthia said some cutting things…"

"Leave it out, Victor. You know full well your mother deliberately tried to get rid of it. You can't accidentally hurl a cat into a passing pickup; it must have taken some welly to turn Kouneli into a feline projectile," Barry retorted. Stomping back into the house, he left me trailing in his wake.

Doreen, Marigold and Moira were lined up like a reception committee in the chilly hallway, desperate to know what was going on without bothering to step outside. No doubt my mother, along with Norman and the Hancocks, was sensibly hogging the fire rather than concerning themselves with an all-too-common cat fight.

"Cynthia's cat has come back," Barry announced gleefully, struggling to keep hold of the writhing, soggy creature. The vile cat's back arched in indignation and it hissed like a thing possessed: extending a claw, it viciously scratched Barry's face, drawing blood.

"Get that thing out of here, Barry," Doreen cried, callously ignoring his bleeding face. "The damn thing's a menace."

"Have a bit of heart, Doreen. He's been on the missing list for weeks," Barry responded.

"I wish it still was. It's not welcome in my home. Last time it snuck in it tried to have its wicked way with my Tickles."

"I thought Tickles was a Tom," Marigold said.

"Well, that didn't stop the pervert," Doreen retorted. "Not only did it leave poor Tickles with a bloody ear, he was so traumatised that he took to hiding under the duvet for weeks. Norman had to move into the spare bedroom with his traffic cones, he refuses to sleep with Tickles."

"Just be thankful that it didn't manage to impregnate your cat like it did to my poor Clawsome," Marigold said.

"I think that would have been physically impossible," I pointed out pedantically.

The door flew open and Gordon walked in,

cradling Waffles in his arms as though the soppy mutt had lost the use of its legs.

"Waffles. Whatever has happened to him?" Moira was close to hyperventilating.

"That cat attacked him," Gordon accused, pointing at the wriggling culprit still struggling to free itself from Barry's firm grasp.

"I'd best take Kouneli home," Barry said. "Cynthia and Anastasia will be tickled pink to be reunited with him. I don't suppose you've got a cat basket I could borrow, Doreen. Cynthia will skin me alive if I lose him on the way home."

Frowning sulkily, Doreen begrudgingly dug out a cat basket and rushed Barry out before venting her annoyance at having a damp dog in her hallway. "I draw the line at wet dogs indoors. I think you should take it home before it stinks the place out."

"Again," I laughed.

"Trust you to find it funny, Victor. You have the most warped sense of humour," Doreen clucked.

"Actually the dog smells quite nice, he has quite a perfumed aroma," Marigold said. I found my wife's tactics glaringly transparent. Whilst she has never demonstrated the slightest fondness for dogs, she was obviously flattering Waffles to make a favourable impression on Moira.

"That will be the lavender shampoo I washed

him with earlier," Moira explained. "You should never have made us put him out in the garden, Doreen. Waffles looks totally bedraggled. I'll have to take him to the grooming parlour…."

"Never mind the state of his coat," Gordon interrupted. "That vicious cat had its claws into him and may have done some damage under his curls."

"Oh, goodness. I think you'd better rustle up a first aid kit, Doreen," Moira pleaded.

Watching Moira attempt to patch up the bedraggled and traumatised yelping animal, I reassessed my opinion that the dog wasn't frightened of cats: at least if it wasn't scared of them before its encounter with Kouneli, it would likely be terrified of them now.

Chapter 10

Raiding the Fray Bentos Stash

I t's hard to credit that mangy cat had the sense to find its way home. Still, it should put a stop to that Cynthia's snivelling. The way she carried on about it, anyone would think I did it deliberate," Violet Burke huffed indignantly as we made our way home from the dinner party at a suitable pace to accommodate her swollen feet. "'Appen I should have slung the blasted thing into a pickup that had further to go. Who'd have thunk it could make it's way home?"

I smiled at the irony of my mother's words, regretting she hadn't managed to send Kouneli on a longer trip whilst simultaneously professing her innocence of hurling the cat out on purpose.

Once again balaclaved up, Violet Burke clutched a Tupperware box stuffed full of Charlotte Russe to her sturdy bosom, having practically snatched the leftovers out of the hands of the impoverished Hancocks, the intended recipients of Doreen's boxed up largesse. Edna had silently fumed at my mother's greed, but considering Edna's habit of feeding any old scraps to her cats, Violet Burke had likely done the felines a favour, protecting their digestive systems from an overload of cream: it certainly disagreed with Marigold's pampered imported domestics. Hopefully, my mother's declaration that, "This will go nicely with a mucky fat toastie if I get peckish in the night," would go some way towards knocking her off Milton's pedestal. It was hard to envisage anyone fantasising over a lard smeared Violet Burke.

"I really like Moira, I felt an instant connection between us," Marigold said, squeezing my arm.

"I know what you mean, lass. I took to her myself right off the bat." Their words brought another smile to my face. It was rare for my wife and my mother to so readily agree about anything. "She's a damn sight less stingy with the wages she's offering than that Doreen is. With all the airs and graces she gives herself, you wouldn't have Doreen down as a right mucky bugger but you should see the state of her kitchen."

"I think that's down to Norman. You ought to invite Doreen to join you on your furniture shopping spree, Marigold. She won't appreciate being left out." It struck me that with Norman destined to spend his every waking moment experimenting with fancy cakes, Doreen might find herself at a loose end. She could well turn into a secret tippler if she ended up playing second fiddle to Moira.

"Don't be silly, Victor. Anyone would think from the way that you talk that Doreen and I are joined at the hip..."

"Well, I can barely turn round at home without tripping over the blasted woman. She's never off the doorstep." Considering this was true, I realised I had scored a bit of an own goal in encouraging Marigold to keep Doreen close.

"Oh, how you do exaggerate, Victor," Marigold scoffed. "Can you try and speed it up a bit, Vi. We really need to be getting back to our houseguests."

"It'll be on your head if my feet explode. I expect that I caught a nasty dose of chilblains tonight. That Doreen wants her head examined, expecting us to eat outside in all weathers with nowt but a bit of flippin plastic..."

"I think flapping would be more apt," I chortled.

My mother's grumbling washed over me as we slowly progressed through the village. Fortunately, it had stopped drizzling and the clear night sky hinted we could be in for good weather the next day.

"'Appen I'll come up and say hello…" Vi said as we finally reached the *apothiki*.

"Not advisable, Mother. I want you to keep well clear until we can get shot of them tomorrow…"

"Anyone would think you're ashamed of me, lad."

"Perish the thought. It's just that Emily and Bill were neighbours of ours back in Manchester and saw you hanging around at our old address when you first decided to come and find me. They heard you shouting the odds and insisting you were the new owner's mother despite all his protestations to the contrary," I explained.

"Don't talk daft, lad. It's nigh on two years since the Sally Army sent me that address in Manchester. Your visitors will hardly remember me after all that time."

"Actually, Mother, you made such a memorable impression that they gave us a blow-by-blow account about your performance earlier…their description of you fitted to a tee." Sparing my mother's feelings, I neglected to mention that Bill had described her as a deranged old harridan, vulgar and common to boot.

"Cor, they must have dull lives if they've nothing else to talk about but summat and nowt from two year back."

"Well, tongues may well start wagging if our visitors start questioning how the mother that Gary publicly disowned has now turned out to be mine. Just slip off to Doreen's first thing in the morning and keep out of sight."

Persuaded by my logic, Vi admitted, "Aye, lad, when you put it like that. Best if I keep out of your hair till you've got rid. I don't want folk here judging me if it came out about that whole baby in a bucket thing."

"Not to mention the pink frilly bonnet," I muttered under my breath.

"You do know that I'm right glad that fellow in Manchester wasn't you in the end? He was a bit common, like."

My mother's words brought a lump to my throat. It was a pity she had to go and ruin the moment by adding, "I was hard pressed to work out who his father could have been. He didn't have the look of any of the fellas I'd been a bit free with."

"Well, I am glad that you finally found me," I told her as she let herself into the *apothiki*.

"Goodnight then, Vi." Marigold pecked my

mother on the balaclava before taking my hand. Leaning in close, she planted a warm kiss on my cold cheek as I gazed upstairs for any sign of our unwanted visitors burning the midnight oil. "Try to put a brave face on it, Victor. They're only here for one night."

"Don't forget we'll be saddled with them for lunch tomorrow," I reminded her.

"Well, I doubt it could be any more tedious than that ghastly dinner we just sat through. If Doreen had warned me that we'd been dining al-fresco, I would have invested in some thermal underwear."

Creeping indoors like a couple of teenagers not wanting to be caught out breaking curfew, we were relieved to see that all the lights were out. It appeared that our visitors had retired for the night, an assumption corroborated by the sound of snoring drifting out from the guest bedroom.

"Let's have a quick coffee and a nightcap, darling," Marigold suggested. Walking into the kitchen, she exclaimed, "It looks as though someone has had a good time."

"At my expense," I observed, noting the three empty wine bottles lined up on the kitchen table. "It seems they raided my supply of good Lidl wine. They must have had a good rummage. I deliberately hid it at the back of the cupboard behind the cheap plastic plonk."

"Well, there's no sign that they made themselves anything to eat. Since it looks as though they went to bed without any dinner, I'd better pull out all the stops and make them a decent breakfast tomorrow," Marigold sighed.

"How about a full English?"

I couldn't remember the last time that Marigold had allowed me to enjoy a good fry-up. Her claim that such fare was nothing short of a heart attack on a plate was at odds with her own propensity for indulging her sweet tooth with calorific custard laden *bougatsas* and pistachio *halvah*. Lately, I was happy enough to suffer the fried bacon ban without complaint, Violet Burke being more than amenable to sneaking me the odd bacon butty when I popped downstairs. Naturally, I didn't mention it to my wife: there was no point in raising Marigold's blood pressure by having her unduly worrying about my cholesterol levels.

"Don't be silly, Victor. Our guests haven't travelled across the continent for a full English. They'll be expecting nothing less than a traditional Greek breakfast."

"So, Greek coffee and cigarettes all round..."

"Very droll. We can squeeze some fresh juice; there are plenty of oranges on the tree..."

"If Guzim hasn't picked it clean."

"And you could knock up that scrambled egg thing you do with tomatoes and feta…"

"*Strapatsada.*"

"That's it. And there's Greek yoghurt and honey.

"*Giaoutri kai meli…*"

"I just opened a new tin of that delicious honey that Giannis gave us…"

"The wildflower one. It's far too good to waste on our visitors," I said churlishly, reluctant to spare even a spoonful of the exquisite nectar on a couple unlikely to spot the difference between superior organic local honey scented with natural wildflowers and the cheap stuff that came in a squeezy bottle.

Opening the dishwasher to deposit the wine glasses used by our visitors, I nearly dropped the glassware in shock at the sight of two empty Fray Bentos tins neatly stacked in the plate rack. Bill and Emily must have dug to the very back of our cupboards to help themselves to my very limited supply of the traditional British delicacy. I had been careful to stash my secret supply well out of Marigold's sight behind a row of dented Greek tins which Tina had fobbed me off with in part payment of my wages.

"Darling, what was that you were saying about them expecting Greek food in Greece?" I chortled, drawing Marigold's attention to the empty tins.

"I don't understand. Whoever heard of anyone washing and saving used Fray Bentos tins rather than just binning them? It's very odd behaviour," Marigold noted.

"According to my Mother, it is all the rage in Warrington. One of her chippy regulars saved them up to use as feeding bowls for his ferrets."

"I expect Vi was pulling your leg, Victor."

"Nonsense, she saves her own. She swears blind they turn out excellent Yorkshire puddings." I was relieved that Marigold was focusing on the empty tins rather than interrogating me about my secret stash of pies. My relief was short lived.

"Where on earth did they get their hands on Fray Bentos?"

"Perhaps they brought them over in their luggage."

"Are you keeping something from me? I'd be very disappointed to learn they were yours after we agreed to stick to a healthy Greek diet."

"If you must know, I like to keep a few in for emergencies," I confessed.

"A pie emergency!"

"I may need to feed my mother if she pops in unexpectedly…"

"Shush, I heard something."

Following Marigold as she moved to the doorway to investigate, I pointed towards the bathroom door at the tell-tale sound of the toilet flushing. I stifled an involuntary chuckle at the sight of Bill emerging clad in nothing but a short floral satin robe straining over his paunch. Clearly still half-comatose from the amount of my wine he had knocked back, he stumbled into the spare bedroom, unaware of our presence.

"What a flaming cheek," Marigold hissed. "That was my robe."

"It looks much better on you, darling," I assured her. "Bill really doesn't have the figure for it."

Chapter 11

Guzim is no Tony Curtis

Marigold was up with the lark for once. I barely had chance to down my first coffee before she was fussing around, setting the table with a veritable spread of olives and home-made jams to impress our guests. Slapping my hands away from the olives, she shooed me out, sending me off to collect a freshly baked batch of Dina's home-made bread. Dina never missed her Friday tradition of preparing enough bread in the outside oven to keep the taverna going for a week and supply the village needs.

The day looked promising with clear blue skies

and a hint of sunshine on the horizon. Squinting into the distance, the sea appeared calm. Shrugging off my annoyance at the prospect of having lunch with our home intruders, I decided to make the most of it: a midday drive down to Neo Itilo could well turn out to be a pleasant outing.

With no one around at such an early hour to pass the time of day with, my progress to the taverna was swift. Arriving at the taverna, I smiled at the sight of Dina busy outside. Wrapped up against the early morning chill, she sported a voluminous flour splattered apron above her thick winter jacket, a few stray hairs peeking out from beneath the dark green head scarf neatly knotted under her chin. Hearing my approach, Dina straightened up from tending the oven. Stretching, she kneaded her back to iron out the knots, greeting me warmly with a kiss, instructing me to come, sit and have a coffee. "*Elate, kathiste, piete enan kafe.*" Dragging a chair close to the heat of the *fournos* she remarked that I was earlier than the Greeks, "*Eisai noritera apo tous Ellines.*"

Grabbing hold of an ancient looking implement resembling a metal shovel with a long wooden handle, Dina retrieved a humongous round loaf from the *fournos,* deftly sliding it onto a table.

Hoping to expand my Greek vocabulary with the addition of a no doubt obscure term, I asked her what the tool was called. *"Ti legatai afto to ergaleio?"*

"Einai ena ftyari," she replied, telling me it was a shovel.

"Have you never to see the shovel before?" Nikos laughed as he emerged from the taverna, his hearty slap on my back taking the wind out of me.

"Of course I have. I just thought the implement would have a more exotic sounding name because of the long history of wood-ovens."

"Exoticos." Nikos doubled over in laughter at the absurdity, sharing the joke with Dina before she disappeared inside to make coffee. "You want the exotic tool, I let you to use the *tsounkrana elias*. You know what he is, yes?"

"It's an olive rake…"

"I let you to use him. You come to help with the olive, yes?" Nikos' eyes twinkled with amusement. I was more than familiar with Nikos' incessant attempts to convince me to help with his harvest, unsuccessfully selling it as a quintessential Greek experience not to be missed.

"Nice try, Niko, but you'll have to make do with Guzim. I've only come to collect the bread."

"How you can to live the Greek life with no experience of the olive?" he teased.

"You know full well that I helped Dimitris with his harvest…"

"Po, Dimitri just play at the olive. He is the

amateur, he only have the fifty tree," Nikos scoffed.

"Fifty…I didn't realise he had so many," I admitted. I had spent the best part of a morning getting hands-on experience of the olive harvest by helping Dimitris out a couple of weeks earlier. A couple of trees had been more than enough to satisfy my curiosity, confirming my suspicion that it was back-breaking work. I recalled that Dimitris had appeared a tad taken aback that I took the opportunity to slink away when it started to rain. If he had been expecting me to hang around to strip the fruit from the other forty-eight trees, he might have mentioned it. Then again, he is always unfailingly polite and he could hardly take umbrage considering that I had volunteered my help.

"The fifty is the nothing. I have more than the thousand and half tree," Nikos boasted.

Dina emerged from the taverna carrying a laden tray containing a shallow bowl of olive oil, three coffees and two glasses of water. Nikos extended one of the glasses to me: knocking back the contents of his own glass, he said, "*Ela*, Victor. It will to put the hair on the chest," disillusioning me of the notion that the glass contained water.

"What is it?" I enquired warily.

"*Tispouro.*"

"It's a bit early in the day for me," I declined, having no intention of following in Norman's recent path as a day tippler.

Breaking a piece of bread from the cooling loaf, Nikos dipped it in olive oil, a look of bliss transforming his features as he chewed.

As we huddled around the welcoming warmth of the oven, the village slowly came to life around us. A local tooted his horn as he flew by on his moped, an olive rake precariously balanced over one shoulder. Litsa appeared in her garden opposite the taverna, waving her walking stick at us before using it to knock a few oranges from the high branches.

"How are you getting along having my mother cleaning the taverna?" I asked Nikos.

"The Dina love the Violet. With the Violet to cleaning, the Dina have the no work to do..."

"*Ti les*?" Hearing her name, Dina asked her husband what he was saying.

As Nikos dutifully translated, painting her as a lady of leisure, she openly scoffed. Turning on her husband, she reminded him that although Violet relieved her from slopping the mop around the taverna, *she* was still responsible for all the housework. Nikos hung his head as Dina complained that on top of that, she helped him in the fields on a daily basis before spending her evenings cooking in the taverna.

"*Alla i Violet xefloudizei tis patates,*" Nikos fired

back, saying Violet peeled the potatoes.

"Well, I can say from experience that baking the bread for the village is dastardly hard work," I said.

"So, you found the woman work too challenging, Victor? The bread making is not the work, Dina do it ever since we marry," Nikos countered. I marvelled at the thought of Dina repeating the same chore for decades, upholding a tradition she could easily have sacked off with the advent of supermarket shelves brimming with sliced bread. Instead, she maintained the ritual, taking pride in her craft. It saddened me to think that the tradition was unlikely to outlast Dina's generation. I doubted today's youngsters would be willing to roll out of bed before dawn to follow in Dina's footsteps when they could simply chuck a packet mix from Lidl into an electric bread maker. I must confess that the novelty of grappling with my own outside oven that Barry had knocked up for me, had soon worn off.

Downing his coffee and the second glass of lethal spirit, Nikos winked at me. "I need this before a day with the Guzim. The real work is the putting up with the your Albanian."

"He's not actually mine," I pointed out. The villagers' constant references to Guzim as 'my Albanian' made him sound like my pet.

"There you are, Victor. I can't think what took you

so long," Marigold complained when I returned with the bread.

"I had to wait for the loaf to bake," I said, neglecting to mention that I had hung around drinking coffee with Nikos. Gesticulating towards the guest bedroom, I added, "Are they up yet?"

"I think Emily's still in the shower...ah, here's Bill now. Good morning, Bill, did you sleep well?" As Marigold spoke, her expression lightened from one of annoyance to amusement. Whilst she was no doubt justifiably irritated to discover Bill prancing into the kitchen in nothing but her floral satin robe, it was hard not to be amused by the ridiculous figure he cut.

"Like a log. Your guestroom is very comfortable," Bill said, self-consciously smoothing the short skirt of Marigold's robe against his thighs whilst tightening the belt over his paunch. Paired with black knee socks, the robe left Bill's hairy legs on full display.

"I've just been flashed by a horrible little man in his underpants. He was washing himself down with a hosepipe at the bottom of your garden," Emily announced as she entered the kitchen.

"Well, technically he didn't flash you if he kept his underpants on," I pointed out, thinking at least Guzim hadn't removed his underwear which was more than could be said for Bill, who was flashing his dangly bits around beneath Marigold's robe. I couldn't resist a sarcastic dig: "And it should reassure you that vulgar neighbours are not unique to the Close."

"I do wish that Guzim would shower behind that curtain I tacked up on the side of his shed?" Marigold said.

"Guzim? So you know the near-naked man?" Emily accused.

"Of course we do. We draw the line at randoms infiltrating the garden to strip down to their underwear. I'd be out there shooing him off if he wasn't my gardener."

"He's from Albania," Marigold added as if that made it all perfectly normal. In a way, of course, it had become the new normal for us. It was rare for any of Guzim's bizarre habits to surprise us these days. If Marigold had anticipated today was the day for Guzim's weekly shower, she may have persuaded me to pop down and convince him to give it a miss until the house was free of visitors.

"The bathroom's free, Bill," Emily prompted her husband, belatedly realising he wasn't suitably attired for the breakfast table. With Bill out of the way, Marigold and Emily chatted whilst I whipped up my signature *strapatsada* and popped some of Dina's freshly baked bread under the grill to toast.

I was relieved to see that Bill had donned some

clothes when he returned to the kitchen just as I was plating the eggs. "I didn't have you down as the sort of fellow to be wearing a pinny," he quipped.

"And I didn't have you down as the sort of fellow to wander round in my wife's satin robe," I retorted.

"Touché. This looks awfully good," Bill said. "I suppose that the Greeks have been breakfasting on such a grand repast since ancient times."

"Not really. Tomatoes didn't arrive in Greece until the nineteenth century and apparently the ancients weren't big fans of eggs. They'd have been more likely to tuck into a handful of olives whilst dipping barley bread into wine."

Bill's eyes lit up with a gleam at the thought of breakfast wine. Ignoring it, I poured him a glass of freshly squeezed orange juice.

"The eggs are from Victor's chickens and the juice is from the oranges on our tree. The strawberry jam is from Victor's latest batch, he had such a glut of strawberries this year," Marigold said with pride.

"Very impressive. You've really embraced the Greek lifestyle. Haven't they done well, Emily?" Bill said, his tone hardly patronising at all.

"They have," she agreed.

"You could always keep hens in Manchester or would that be lowering the tone?"

"Horrible smelly creatures," Emily pronounced,

her attempt to muster a look of disgust impeded by the Botox.

"I make Victor keep his downwind," Marigold said. "For some unfathomable reason, he's very fond of them and treats them like pets."

"We can't have pets tying us down," Bill said.

"Now that Bill's retired, we plan to take lots of holidays," Emily explained.

"I suppose you have to go to the expense of putting your hens into kennels if you want to get away," Bill pondered.

"No need for that," I replied, resisting the urge to mock his suggestion that chickens were shipped off to kennels. "We've got Guzim."

As we tucked into breakfast, Bill told us that they had spent the previous evening pouring over a map of the area between here and Sparta. *While you were pouring my wine down your gullet*, I thought without voicing it.

"Bill's always wanted to go to Sparta, he's such a huge fan of the film," Emily said.

"The film?"

"'Spartacus'," Bill said.

"Tony Curtis was lovely in that. So handsome," Marigold cooed.

"Oh, wasn't he," Emily nodded in agreement. "Have you seen the restored version, Marigold? They added an originally censored scene with a half-naked Tony Curtis in the bath."

"So, Emily, I take it you wouldn't have objected to a half-naked Tony Curtis hosing himself off in my garden."

As I pointed out her hypocrisy, Emily had the grace to blush whilst Marigold quipped, "Guzim is no Tony Curtis."

"Anyway, what has the film 'Spartacus' got to do with you wanting to go to Sparta?" I asked Bill.

"Spartacus was a Spartan warrior…" Bill said.

"Where on earth did you get that idea? Spartacus was originally a slave from Thrace who led a revolt against the Romans back in 72BC. The Spartans were about 300 years earlier," I pointed out.

"Are you sure?" Bill looked a tad deflated to have been caught out fudging his history.

"Victor spends hours with his nose buried in dusty old tomes on Greek history," Marigold said. "He needs to keep up to date on his history because he reps in the summer."

"Well as long as Sparta is famous for something it's worth a look-see, isn't it Bill," Emily said.

"It's definitely worth exploring for its history," Marigold said, sending a blistering look in my direction for bursting Bill's 'Spartacus' bubble.

Looking at Bill's downturned lip, I felt a twinge of guilt. "The Maniots in this area are descended from Ancient Spartans and claim to have warrior blood coursing through their veins."

"That's fascinating." Bill immediately perked up at this historical titbit. "Do you have many warrior type neighbours?"

"Well, most of them are a bit past all that now," I said, thinking that Panos had certainly demonstrated the warrior spirit when he had turned up at the police station ready to give it a bit of welly if it had been needed to secure to my release. "I haven't seen it but the film 'Troy' was released earlier this year. I believe it's about the war between Troy and Sparta."

Immediately cheered at this news, Bill said, "We must see if it's on at the cinema when we get home. I can't wait to take in all the sights at Sparta and then watch the original war on the big screen. Now, what was that place you suggested we meet you for lunch?"

"Neo Itilo. It's only a tiny village but there are a couple of restaurants right by the sea."

"That's it. When we perused the map yesterday evening we spotted a Fort near there. We thought we'd explore it this morning before we meet up with you later."

"Kefala Fort. You should enjoy it. It's above old Itilo. The views down to the coast from up there are truly magnificent."

"Excellent. We'll explore the fort, have lunch by

the sea and then head down to Sparta. Anything worth seeing on the way?"

"It's worth making a stop at Gythio..."

"You must find it very handy, Marigold, being married to a tour guide," Emily said.

"Well, I've learnt to tune out when he starts regurgitating the same dreary facts every time we drive anywhere. I had plenty of practice after years of him droning on about hygiene regulations." Marigold attempted to soften her words by adding, "Just teasing, darling."

Chapter 12

Easy Peas and a Piece of Cake

Squashing their luggage into the hire car, Bill insisted that we synchronise our watches to ensure we wouldn't be late meeting them for lunch. Before driving off to explore, the couple launched a last ditch effort to try and persuade us to join them in trailing round the ruined fort. Fortunately Marigold came up with a plausible get-out clause to avoid an extra encounter, claiming she couldn't possibly miss the monthly meeting to beautify the cemetery. There was almost a hint of reverence in her voice as Marigold declared in a saccharine tone, "I consider it my duty to give back to my adopted village."

I suppressed an ironic smile at her words. Marigold regularly came up with the unlikeliest excuses to escape her weeding duties. Preferring to avoid any actual grubbing around in the dirt on her knees, she had a tendency to turn up late, just in time to enjoy the social aspect of drinking coffee and eating cake. Whilst in principle Marigold was all for mucking in, she was less than enthusiastic in practice.

Waving the pair off, Marigold lamented, "I'll never be able to wear that robe again. I suppose you may as well give it to Guzim, he's forever pestering you for cast-offs."

"I think even Guzim may baulk at the idea of prancing round in a short floral number..."

"He really ought to get over his objection to pink. I do believe it's becoming all the rage in gentlemen's fashion. I think you could get away with a delicate shade now that you're clean shaven again."

"I rather doubt that Guzim has any pretensions of being a gentleman," I pointed out, ignoring her suggestion that I incorporate pink into my wardrobe. Being more than capable of selecting my own button downs, I have never been the sort of husband who relies on my wife to dress me.

"Are you really going off to beautify the cemetery?"

"I suppose I ought to show willing. I do hope

the ground isn't too muddy after last night's drizzle. I've no time to do a cake though. Be a dear and pop over to the shop and see if there's something I can pass off as home-made."

"I don't know why you want to bother. I expect that Norman has been up since dawn knocking up some classic French gateaux for Doreen to take along."

"If Doreen's going to start playing the game of one-upmanship, at least I can say that I make my own and don't rely on you to create my cakes and biscuits." Whilst Marigold is indeed the baker in our kitchen, the irony of her sending me off to purchase shop bought cake was lost on her. "Now, do run along to the shop," she wheedled before returning indoors.

Ambling across the village square, I looked on the bright side. With Marigold off beautifying the cemetery, my time was my own until lunchtime. I determined to put the hours to good use by preparing for my next cookery class. It would be a novel event, involving travelling to someone else's kitchen. Word of my classes had reached other expats living outside Meli who were keen to get to grips with the fine art of Greek cooking. I had just accepted an invitation to host a class in a village some fifteen kilometres distant. Whilst a tad apprehensive about demonstrating my skills in an unfamiliar kitchen in front of a bunch of strangers, the money on offer was not to be sniffed at.

Making my way home with a hastily selected packet of *Gemista* chocolate biscuits going cheap since they were long past their sell-by date, I wondered if Marigold was up to the challenge of passing them off as home-made. It would take more than her customary sprinkling of icing sugar to convince our Greek neighbours that the likely stale contents of the recognisable branded packet were fresh from the oven.

I needn't have worried: Marigold, deep in conversation on the telephone was oblivious to my choice. Shamelessly eavesdropping on my wife's conversation, my heart sank when she finished the call by saying, "You can't let an opportunity like that slip by. Pop round now and Victor can drive you, he's nothing else on this morning."

"Drive exactly who to where?" I demanded.

Ignoring my question, Marigold relieved me of the biscuits. Tutting in dismay, she said, "It's a good job I won't need these after all, they're a terrible choice. I may as well come along with you..."

"Come along with me where?"

"Let me just give Athena a ring and let her know I won't be able to join the ladies in the cemetery."

Frustrated by her deliberate attempt to avoid

my questions, I retired to the balcony to take a deep breath.

"What is going on, Marigold?" I asked when she finished catching up on all the gossip with Athena and joined me outside.

"Oh, didn't I mention? You're taking Gordon and Moira to the police station. You need to help them sort out their residency permits…"

"No, I'm not. Spiros is going to take care of all that. There's no rush…"

"But there is. Gordon needs it sorting urgently because he's found a second-hand car and the owner has only promised to hold it for him until tomorrow. He's in a bit of a panic at the thought of losing it."

I was surprised to hear that Gordon was taking a risk by considering opting for a used car rather than new. When he asked my advice about acquiring a suitable vehicle, I had cautioned it was a bit rash to splurge his cash on a used vehicle of unknown provenance. I pointed out that the second-hand car market in Greece was vastly overpriced due to the Greeks not bothering with the concept of depreciation. Nevertheless, it appeared that Gordon had disregarded my recommendation that he visit the Punto dealership in town, preferring instead to plump for a second-hand car or a *metacheirismeno aftokinito* as it is known in Greek.

"It's a bit out of my comfort zone," I objected, having no desire to show my face in the police station so soon after my recent spell in the cells: the very thought of it made me squirm. "Let me try and get hold of Spiros, he's the man to sort it."

Spiros proved to be no use at all. Answering his mobile, he explained, "I already tell the Gordon you must to go with him for the *karta adeias diamonis*. I have the emergency."

"A sudden death?" I enquired, a reasonable assumption considering Spiros' profession.

"I hope very much not the death but the Nikos he make the lot of blood in the hearse…"

"You've lost me, Spiro. I don't understand."

"I take the Nikos to the hospital…"

"But I was with him less than an hour ago, he was perfectly healthy then."

"There is the accident with the olives…with the how you say, the *prioni*?"

"The saw."

As Spiros spoke, I could hear Nikos loudly cursing Guzim as a clumsy oaf in the background: losing blood seemingly hadn't affected his ability to vent his rage about the wretched Albanian. Recalling that Nikos had knocked back two generous glasses of *tsipouro* before setting off for the morning's work, I wondered if he was unfairly maligning Guzim. Since the birth of his son and heir, Fatos, the

Albanian shed dweller had knocked his habit of downing a breakfast beer on the head, thus demonstrating a much more responsible attitude than Nikos towards working with dangerous tools.

Before I could elicit any details from Spiros regarding Nikos' injury, he assured me, "I give to the Gordon the list of the paper he need. It will be, how you to say in the English, the easy peas...the piece of pie."

"It's easy-peasy and a piece of cake," I corrected, certain that procuring official Greek papers would be neither.

"Thelis kafe? Tha stathmefso sto pezodromio," Spiros said.

Spiros was making no sense: he had just asked me if I wanted coffee before saying he was parking on the pavement. "Why are you asking me if I want coffee? I thought you were on your way to the hospital."

"Not the you, I ask the Nikos if he want coffee. I telephone to you later from the hospital."

Before disconnecting the call, I heard Spiros shouting at Nikos to watch where the blood dripped as he'd just had the hearse cleaned. I supposed that if Nikos was capable of downing a takeaway coffee, he could hardly be at death's door.

Staring at the receiver in exasperation, I wondered how I could wriggle my way out of accompanying Gordon to the police station. Although I had tagged along with Spiros to various offices to acquire endless reams of paperwork adorned with official Greek stamps, I remained oblivious to what most of the papers were for. I had certainly never ventured into the bureaucratic arena alone. To be frank, I wasn't sure that I was up to the task.

"There's no point trying to squirm out of it, Victor. After all you were happy enough to take Gordon's commission for helping him to make the move to Greece," Marigold said.

"The commission was for finding him a house," I pointed out.

"And for acting as a go-between to navigate the Stranges through the uncharted course of Greek bureaucracy," Marigold reminded me.

"Yes, but tagging along with Spiros, not alone. Anyway, we've arranged to meet Emily and Bill for lunch," I prevaricated.

"There's plenty of time, we don't need to set off to Itilo until midday. Now do get a move on, there they are now." Marigold nearly poked my eye out, waving frantically at the Stranges.

"Why are you so keen to come along?" I quizzed.

"I'm sure Moira will appreciate the company."

"Not to mention it gets you out of weeding a muddy graveyard," I said.

BUCKET TO GREECE (VOL.10)

Reluctantly following Marigold down to the street, I consoled myself with the thought that with any luck a major crime might be underway: such a fortuitous event would leave the police with no time to deal with providing pesky paperwork to law-abiding foreigners.

I noticed that Gordon was suitably prepared with the large box file containing every last document he had acquired since the move. I shuddered at the thought of being expected to identify the relevant paperwork needed for the permits. I hadn't got a clue which of my many papers Spiros had handed over to the police for my own application. I had been more than happy to leave it all in his capable hands, simply coughing up an endless supply of small change to pay for the multitude of photocopies that ensured every paper was presented in triplicate. As an aside, I remember being quite fascinated by the sheer number of photocopying shops hidden away on every back street in town, rivalling the number of charity shops and estate agents proliferating in small English towns.

"Moira's got the dog with her," I exclaimed. "I really don't want that creature shedding hairs all over the Punto."

"Don't show me up by making a fuss about it…" Marigold warned, determined to make a good impression on her new friend.

Greeting Gordon, I noticed Moira having to coax Waffles along. Resisting the tugs on its lead, it appeared reluctant to join us. Moira had nearly dragged it as far as the car when it refused to budge a step further. Hanging its head, a visible tremor ripped through its body before it unleashed a gaseous explosion replicating the one of the previous evening.

"Poor Waffles, his stomach is still a trifle unsettled," Moira said. Moving forward to have a good sniff of the Punto's rear tyre, the dog whimpered piteously before evacuating its bowels, only just missing the Punto's bodywork.

"I hope he feels better after that," Moira said. Rushing into action with a poopa scoopa, she bagged up the mess. "I'm so worried about Waffles getting sick in the car."

"Probably best to leave it behind then," I suggested, adding for good measure, "I doubt that the police will allow dogs in the police station."

"He's a he, not an it; I can't just leave him behind," Moira said. "Anyway, Spiros said it made sense for us both to get our residence permits at the same time so I'll have to come along."

"Perhaps we could leave Waffles with someone in the village," Gordon suggested.

Mulling his words, I realised I'd just been offered a get out of jail card. "I suppose that I could walk Waffles round the village while Marigold goes with you to sort out the papers."

"But your Greek is better than mine, Victor, and I'm clueless about paperwork." Marigold's words dashed my hopes of getting off the hook so easily.

The Stranges stared with interest as the black clad figure of Kyria Maria emerged from her house. The elderly woman narrowly avoided tripping over the trailing dog lead, almost dropping the cake tin she was clutching.

"*Ti einai afto?*" Pointing at Waffles, Maria asked what it was.

"*Einai ena chryso poodle.*" Still oblivious to the correct translation of a goldendoodle, I told my neighbour it was a golden poodle.

"*Einai diki sas?*" Maria asked if it was mine.

"*Ochi, anikei stous filous mou.*" Gesturing towards Gordon and Moira, I told Maria that it belonged to my friends.

A smile transformed Maria's wrinkled features. Bending down to pet the dog, she proclaimed it was very beautiful. "*Einai poly omorfo.*"

A germ of an idea began to form in my brain; perhaps I could palm the mutt off on Maria rather than risk it stinking out the Punto. Whilst she was clearly not a responsible choice, my overriding concern was ensuring the Punto remained free of dog sick and other bodily waste. Hoping Maria would rise to the bait, I told her that we needed someone to look after the dog, saying we had to go the police station. *"Chreiazomaste kapoion na frontisei to skyli. Prepei na pame sto astynomiko tmima."*

"Giati, eisai enklimatias?" Maria asked 'Why, was I a criminal?'

"Ochi." My denial was adamant.

"Syllifthikes prin." It was hard to deny Maria's observation that I had been arrested before since she had been peering out of her window when I had been carted away in the cop car.

Nevertheless, I managed a suitable comeback, pointing out that it was for working on a Sunday, *"Gia ergasia tin Kyriaki."*

In faltering Greek, Marigold rushed to my defence, pointing out to Kyria Maria that her own son worked on a Sunday too and it didn't make him a criminal: *"Kai o gios sou ergazetai episis tin Kyriaki kai den ton kanei enklimatia."*

Taken aback by Marigold's logic, Kyria Maria volunteered to look after the dog, saying at least it would get her out of beautifying the cemetery.

"At this rate Doreen will be weeding the cemetery on her own," Marigold chortled as Moira and Gordon mimed their gratitude to the old woman.

As Maria led the dog into her house, Moira worried, "I do hope Waffles will be okay with her. You don't think she's a bit too frail to manage him?"

"Nonsense, Kyria Maria has no problem at all keeping up with her own pet," I assured her, purposefully neglecting to mention that my old neighbour's pet was a tortoise.

Chapter 13

Flashing the Cash

Although I had been coerced into heading down to the police station against my will, it was impossible not to enjoy the drive simply because of Moira's infectious enthusiasm for everything we passed en route. Since she had only spent a few days in Meli on her previous trip, everything appeared new and exciting to her. As she gushed over landscapes that had become all too familiar, I found myself appreciating them anew through fresh eyes.

As the glistening blue expanse of sea came into view, Moira said wistfully, "Even though the water looks so inviting, I imagine it must be a bit cold to venture in. I doubt that I'll swim until spring."

"You'd have it all to yourself by the look of things," Gordon said.

"You could always brave it on Epiphany," I suggested. "It's traditional for the Greeks to hurl themselves in the sea on the 6th of January..."

"It's quite mad," Marigold added. "After blessing the water, the priest slings in a gold cross and the young men compete to retrieve it..."

"Oh, what fun. Does the winner get to keep it?" Moira asked.

"No such luck. All he gets for his trouble is a poxy blessing. The priest uses the sanctified water for his house blessing ceremonies," I explained.

"The local Papas, Andreas, gave our house a traditional blessing once we'd finished the renovations," Marigold said.

"But he'd run out of sanctified water. We had to settle for the bottled stuff from Lidl," I chortled.

"But he did bless it in my trifle bowl," Marigold reminded me.

Silence descended as Gordon and Moira considered Marigold's words. Even to my ears, the thought of water turning holy after being blessed in a trifle bowl, sounded bizarre, and I'd been there to witness it.

As I drove by a field, Moira exclaimed, "Oh,

look at that poor cow. Its legs are tied together and its udder looks as though it's about to explode.

"I'm afraid that hobbling cows like that is a common practice. It saves the farmer from keeping his herd enclosed…not that you'll spot many cows in these parts. The Greeks aren't that big on beef. Pork tends to be the meat of choice; it's very popular served up as *souvlaki*."

"It's rare to have a steak out that doesn't taste like old shoe leather, I think they use the wrong cut," Marigold said. "Nikos never does steak so I guess it mustn't be an authentic Greek thing."

"I'm just glad that Gordon's given up on all that vegetarian nonsense," Moira laughed. "I can't wait to try Nikos' lamb chops, Gordon was raving about them."

"You know where you are with Nikos' meat," I assured her. "You can be sure it's the genuine article. I heard on the grapevine that a couple of places aren't above passing off goat as lamb; it's cheaper."

"Now, that's your problem, Victor," Marigold piped up.

"I wasn't aware I had one," I retorted.

"You're too attached to those chickens of yours." Expanding her point for the benefit of the Stranges, she explained, "Nikos doesn't go getting all soppy over the animals he rears, whereas Victor won't even hear of me throwing one of his chickens in the pot. He named them all and treats them like pets."

"Well, I think it's important to have pets," Moira said. "Waffles has enhanced our lives no end."

"But chickens aren't pets, they're livestock. Anyway, we've got the cats," Marigold argued.

As Moira clammed up at the mention of cats, Gordon jumped in to cover the awkward silence. "Really appreciate you helping us out. The car that I'm after was just too good an opportunity to pass up."

"I think it's a risk going for a second-hand vehicle," I cautioned.

"But it's not just any old second-hand car. It's a Mazda MX5."

"Can't say that I'm familiar…"

"It's a sports car," Moira volunteered. "I've always fancied one and we've certainly got the climate for it over here. It will be wonderful to drive around with the top down and feel the wind in my hair."

The Punto scraped through a man-made hole stretching across the road, jolting my passengers. Such obstacles were a frequent nuisance, created to facilitate the supply of borrowed electricity when new builds without their own power were going up. My observation was timely. "A sports car doesn't strike me as a very practical choice for these pot-holed roads. Not to mention the roads are prone to flooding during torrential rain."

"We'll put the lid on if the weather is bad," Gordon said dismissively.

I wondered what the Greeks would make of a flashy sports car. Most of my neighbours drove round in or on things held together with nothing more than rust patches and a prayer. Although Panos boasted a brand new pickup, he kept it under wraps, saving it for special occasions rather than flaunting it on a daily basis.

"Really, Victor. A sports car will be such fun," Marigold said.

"Don't go getting any ideas," I warned. "If I'm careful to maintain the Punto in tip-top condition there's no reason why we shouldn't get another two decades out of it. After all, it was brand new when I purchased it."

"Must you be such a kill joy," Marigold chided.

"I suppose a sports car will come in handy if you take the dog out with you. The open top will at least prevent any unpleasant bouts of flatulence from lingering," I said to Gordon. "Now, we're almost there. Everyone put your most law-abiding faces on."

The police station was hardly a hive of activity. The

sergeant, busy dealing with someone else when we arrived, indicated that we should take a seat in the waiting area. As the door to his office was wide open, I was able to observe the sergeant being brow-beaten by an elderly Greek woman only half his size: clad all in black, she bore a striking resemblance to my own neighbour, Kyria Maria, though Maria couldn't boast such a luscious moustache. Relentlessly haranguing the police officer, the woman barely allowed him to get a word in edgeways. Turning a keen ear to the proceedings, I shamelessly eavesdropped, hoping to show off my prowess in Greek by translating the nature of whatever heinous crime she was reporting to my companions.

The woman rattled off her complaints at such speed that I was only able to pick out every third word, *"Karota...lachana...kounoupidi."* Mentally translating the discernible words as carrots, cabbages and cauliflowers, I remained at a loss as to why she was providing the sergeant with her grocery list. As she continued her rant, I picked out another few words, helping me to put her vegetable list into context.

"Pane ola. Prepei na syllaveis ton mi kalo Alvano." I duly translated her words to mean, 'All gone. You must arrest the no good Albanian.'

Finally asserting himself, the sergeant argued

back. Luckily he spoke slowly and clearly to emphasise his points. I was able to understand him easily as he claimed that there was no evidence to arrest the Albanian for stealing the vegetables from her garden: most likely they had been uprooted by an animal. Nevertheless the sergeant dutifully began to type up a report. Remembering his one-fingered stabs at the keyboard from my earlier visit, I settled down for a long wait. I was taken by surprise when barely five minutes passed before he ushered the old woman out of his office, beckoning the four of us in.

Leaning back in his chair, he fumbled for a cigarette in the crumpled packet on his desk. Lighting up in blatant disregard of the 'No Smoking' sign on the wall behind him, he inhaled like a desperate man before removing the report he had been working on from the printer. Watching him rip it to shreds, I surmised he had simply been humouring the old woman. I supposed he had no intention of having his officers' stake out her garden as I think she demanded.

Amazingly, the sergeant appeared to have no recollection of ever encountering me before. On reflection, I supposed that since I was now clean shaven and smartly turned out, I must be unrecognisable from the dissolute figure I had cut on my previous visit, unshaven and sweaty in a blood stained apron.

"*Afto to Angliko zevgari chreiazetai tis adeies para-monis tous.*" The sergeant groaned aloud when I told him 'this English couple need their residency permits.'

"*Echoun ta chartia?*"

"He wants your paperwork," I told Gordon. I must admit to a feeling of smugness: the first hurdle had been overcome, the sergeant understood my Greek. Belatedly recalling that on my last visit I had claimed I didn't understand a word of Greek, I was doubly relieved that the sergeant had no recollection of me.

As Gordon duly handed over his enormous box file, the sergeant flicked through the papers with painstaking slowness, muttering *diavatirio* passport, *diefthynsi* address, and *asfaleia ygeias* health insurance, as he scrutinised each document. I stared with interest at a blank spot on the wall behind the sergeant, realising that Besnik's wanted poster was no longer visibly displayed amid the rogue's gallery of wanted criminals. I pondered the likelihood that its absence meant that Besnik had been apprehended for smuggling weapons across the Albanian border in a truck full of rabbits. I hoped that if he had been arrested, he wouldn't squeal on Guzim's young wife Luljeta for acting as his reluctant decoy spouse.

The smart young policeman who had dragged

me out of the shop for illegally trading on a Sunday, wandered into the sergeant's office, depositing a file on his desk. Firing a curious stare in my direction, he tried to place me; shrugging, he returned to his duties.

Seemingly satisfied with the paperwork that Gordon supplied, the sergeant began to type up the details for his records, barking "*Onoma patera,*" at Gordon.

"He wants to know your father's name," I told him.

"They always want that," Marigold added.

The sergeant fired a stern look in my wife's direction before rattling off another demand. Duly translating, I told Gordon, "He says you need to prove that you have independent means to support yourself. You must show him that you have a balance of 8,000 euros in a Greek bank account."

At least I was confident that this particular requirement would be easily met: I had accompanied Gordon to the bank, translating on his behalf to ascertain if a large sum that he had transferred from England had arrived in his bank account. I recalled Gordon being inordinately pleased that the funds were available, having transitioned smoothly.

"It says 4,000 euros here," Gordon argued, pointing to the note that Spiros had scribbled on the paper outlining the necessary requirements for obtaining a residency permit.

"That's 4,000 each."

"But I've only got 5,000 in the joint account. I drew out the rest so that I'd have cash in hand to pay for a car." Leaning in close, Gordon whispered, "In fact, I've got it on me now, I can show him. It's in my money belt."

At least Moira didn't make him stash a large sum of cash in a pouch in his underpants as Marigold, convinced I would be mugged, had insisted I did.

"Well, cash is certainly king in these parts so I expect that will be fine. Let me just explain."

Thrusting the Stranges' bank book under the sergeant's nose, I told him that there was 5,000 in the bank. "*Yparchoun pente chiliades stin trapezi.*"

"*Sto trapezi*?" The sergeant burst into laughter. I failed to see what was so amusing, the penny only dropping that I had made a basic error when he switched to English. "You say there is money in the table. You mean he is in the bank, yes. You mix up the *trapezi* and the *trapeza*."

"It's easily done," I said, sticking with English. "He's good for the money. He can show you the rest in cash."

"Cash," the sergeant appeared confused.

"*Metrita,*" I duly translated.

"Cash no good. He must to have 8,000 *evro* in

bank," the sergeant insisted.

"I don't understand. I need to prove that I have 8,000 euros and I can do that," Gordon piped up. Standing up, he fumbled under his clothing to access his money belt. Retrieving a fat wad of cash, he duly counted out 3,000 euros.

The sergeant's brow furrowed in anger at the sight of the cash.

"I don't think it's a good idea to flash the cash," I hissed to Gordon. "He probably thinks you are trying to bribe him. He takes a dim view where bribes are concerned."

It seemed I was spot on, the sergeant snapping, "Put him away. The 8,000 must be in bank. You go bank and deposit the cash and come back to show me the 8,000 *evro* in bank."

"It would mean going all the way to the bank in town…it makes no sense…you can see that I have enough funds," Gordon argued.

"See. It there in written rule. You must to prove 4,000 *evro* each person in bank." Pointing at the relevant edict on the residency permit checklist, the sergeant remained unbending.

"How about if you just issue Gordon's permit today? The 5,000 euros in the bank covers the amount needed to obtain one permit," I said. Turning to Gordon, I explained, "You only need one residency permit to buy the car. You can come back another day to sort out Moira's."

"That sounds like the most logical way to proceed," Gordon agreed. "I'd have had the necessary funds in the bank if I hadn't withdrawn the cash for the car. I wonder what numbskull comes up with these stupid rules."

"Ours is not to question why," I said, cringing inwardly as I glanced at the sergeant. Fortunately, numbskull didn't appear to feature in his limited English vocabulary.

Ten minutes later, I sighed with relief as we made our escape from the police station, proud that I had successfully handled my first encounter with Greek bureaucracy single-handed. The day had brightened considerably whilst we had been stuck inside. Retrieving my sunglasses from my shirt pocket, I loosened my tie and rolled up my sleeves, welcoming the sun's warm rays on my skin.

Passing his newly acquired residency permit around, Gordon thanked me profusely for my help.

"You look like a serial killer in that photo. Don't you think that he looks awful?" Moira asked me. As she passed the permit to me, I laughed at the state of the crumpled cardboard document adorned with a damp coffee stain, courtesy of the sergeant's clumsiness.

Squinting at Gordon's ink smeared photo, I reassured him, "It's not too bad. The official Greek stamp obscures most of your features."

"Athens here we come," Gordon said, waving the permit triumphantly.

"What?"

"That's where the sports car is. Don't worry, Victor, the chap who's selling it speaks English so we can manage alone. We've got a taxi booked to take us up to the bus station later to catch the Express through to Athens."

"Well, make sure you take a photocopy of the new permit before you set off. Athens is rife with pickpockets and I don't fancy another trip to the police station for the foreseeable. I could feel that young officer's eyes boring into the back of my head. Let's get out of here quickly before he remembers me."

Chapter 14

A Breathtaking Panorama

When we pulled into Meli, my mother was standing in Kyria Maria's doorway surveying the street, a curmudgeonly expression curdling her features. With blue foam rollers wound in her garishly dyed red hair and arms folded across her solid bosom, she typified the image of the sort of bolshie harridan renowned for populating the early days of Coronation Street.

Firing what sounded more like a command than an invitation at Gordon, Violet Burke barked, "Come through. The mutt's in the garden and

Maria is making a pan of that horrible tea out of twigs."

My mother appeared out of sorts: perchance the mess that Norman had left her to clean up in his kitchen had put a damper on her morning.

As the Stranges alighted from the car, Marigold insisted we had no time to linger, worried we would be late for our lunch date. Since it suited me to avoid being stuck translating, I was happy to comply with Marigold's urging to put my foot down. Communication between my mother and our elderly neighbour remained a mystery to me, neither of them having progressed beyond naming fish in a foreign vocabulary.

Leaving the village, Marigold touched up her lipstick in my rear view mirror, an atrocious habit I deplore because it leaves a blind spot at my rear end. Turning a blind eye to her vanity, I couldn't help smiling at her cheery tone. "What a beautiful day for a drive. I can see why the Stranges fancy a sports car. A day like this is made for driving around with the roof down."

"Don't go getting any daft ideas. Keeping up with the Jones in Meli would mean trading down to a moped," I laughed. "Gordon's choice of car strikes me as impractical to say the least. Where are they going to put the dog? You'd never get on with two baskets of cats in a sports car if we need to take them up to the vet."

"I expect you're right, dear…oh, is that an eagle? Watch out, it looks like it's aiming for the windscreen." Marigold ducked instinctively as the bird of prey swooped down, coming perilously close to the Punto.

"It's a good job that we have a car with a lid on," I quipped.

Even though I doubted that I had heard the last of Marigold's aspirations to trade the Punto in for something flashier, I had no intention of giving in. Whilst my wife is of the firm belief that fluttering her eyelashes will weaken my resolve, her seductive methods have been known to fail miserably: a case in point being that she rarely voices her ambition to sink a swimming pool in our garden these days, having given it up as a lost cause.

"Victor, stop the car," Marigold suddenly cried.

"I can't just stop on a bend," I protested, presuming she was having some kind of lipstick emergency.

"I could swear that was Sherry in that field with a man."

"That is hardly grounds for slamming my brakes on. Besides, you said you don't want to be late for this blasted lunch," I reminded her.

"Really, Victor. I just wanted a closer look. I couldn't be sure if it was your friend Dimitris…I wonder what they were up to in that field."

"I imagine they were enjoying a stroll, it's a beautiful day for it after all."

"Sherry never struck me as the strolling type. I've only ever seen her in heels."

The landscape changed as we headed south, lush olive groves giving way to scrubby terrain, sloping hills dotted with rocks sweeping down in the shadow of Taygetos. Whilst the scenery often appears foreboding and brooding in winter, the aspect was brightened by the day's brilliant sunshine: although not exactly lush, it seemed less barren than it appeared when under a curtain of black storm clouds.

Closing in on our destination, we passed a display of stones at the side of the road: fashioned into images of Grecian heads, they were the work of a local craftsman. Marigold reminded me that we must stop there sometime and purchase a head to adorn the wall by our front door. I wondered if she had been paying attention when I'd explained the custom of warring Maniots nailing up the decapitated heads of their enemies: most likely Marigold considered the chiselled heads were merely a decorative feature with no thought to the brutal and savage history of the Mani.

Rounding a bend in the road, we gasped in awe, wowed by the magnificent vista overlooking the bay of Tsipa: the breathtaking panorama never failing to take our breath away. Ignoring the shortcut that wound through the village of old Itilo, I took the long road leading down to the coast, unable to resist the unparalleled views it offered. As we soared towards the sea, Itilo looked down on us, presenting a timeless fairy tale image of picturesque stone houses with red tiled roofs. Reaching our destination, I pulled off the main road, taking the narrow road running parallel to the sea through Neo Itilo. Parking up on a field opposite the narrow pebbly beach, we walked hand in hand towards the cluster of tavernas overlooking the sea.

"Do try to look as though you're enjoying lunch, Victor," Marigold urged. "You won't need to see Emily and Bill again after this."

"I'm sure the lunch will be excellent." There was no trace of sarcasm in my tone as I thought about the food, but I wisely kept my reservations about the company we were about to suffer to myself. There was no point in riling Marigold up: in fairness, her blundering invitation to our old neighbours had only inconvenienced us for one night.

Out of season, only two of the tavernas were open, both sporting outdoor seating beneath wooden canopies. Emily and Bill had already arrived, claiming a table in my taverna of choice. Simply styled with tables featuring checked tablecloths, the owner had made his mark with welcoming touches: garlands of stringed garlic adorned central poles and baskets of flowering plants sitting atop old wooden wine barrels stood sentinel-like at the entrance.

Our lunch companions immediately began raving about the area, Bill declaring it to be exactly the type of off-the-beaten-track spot he loved to discover. To my surprise, I found myself warming to Bill, won over by his genuine delight in my adopted homeland. After waxing poetic about the area for a good five minutes, he said, "Call me snobbish, but holiday spots overrun with British lager louts hold no appeal. This area is just idyllic, unspoiled by development…"

"And not a lager lout in sight," I said, pointedly raising my eyebrow at Bill's bottle of Amstel.

"Emily is taking the wheel for the next leg of the journey," Bill assured me, gesturing towards his wife's can of Fanta orange. "Now that I've retired, we plan to take lots of winter breaks. I don't do the heat well…"

"It's pretty warm today," Marigold said, basking in the December sunshine.

"But not that cloyingly hot heat that you get in summer: that sort of heat brings me out in a sweaty rash."

"Overly sweaty is not a good look on Bill when

he's already plagued with pulsating mosquito bites," Emily added. Glancing at her immovable face, I wondered if any mosquitoes that sucked on her blood would suffer an instant death courtesy of toxic Botox. I made a mental note to research if Botox was deadly to mosquitoes: a quick jab in my sock area might spare me weeks of scratching, not to mention all that messing about with Marmite.

"There was a lovely fresh breeze up by Kelefa Castle earlier," Bill said.

"We identified the scent of wild sage and thyme. And such pretty wild flowers sprouting up between the rocks…and goats gambolling around," Emily added.

"A couple of big horny buggers gave us a bit of a shock, didn't they Emily? Crept up on us," Bill continued. "Pretty rugged landscape up there…"

"And such views…"

"Imagine them carting all those stones up that great hill on foot," Bill remarked.

"I expect they used donkeys," I said.

"I wouldn't fancy being a donkey hauling one of those great big cannons on my back." My mind boggled at the notion of a donkey bearing the weight of a huge cast iron cannon. "Any idea how long the castle's been there?"

"It was built by the Turks in the late seventeenth century before being seized by the Maniots,"

I told him.

"So it's seen plenty of action, then. No wonder it's a bit of a ruin now."

"Bill snagged his jumper on the strangest looking plant; it looked like an enormous cactus with prickly leaves," Emily said.

"It sounds like a prickly pear plant. In Greek it is known as a *fragoskya*," I revealed. "Being a member of the cacti family, it flourishes on rocky terrain. The leaves are actually edible."

"Have you tried them?" Bill raised his eyebrows as though the idea was ludicrous.

"No, they look a bit prickly for my digestive tract," I admitted.

"And it's awfully tricky to prepare prickly pears," Marigold added.

"Almost as dangerous as messing around with fresh artichokes," I warned.

"Artichoke spikes are lethal to Marigolds, they pierce right through the rubber," Marigold added. I smiled at her words, our guests clueless that my wife went under the pseudonym of Marigold in the book I was covertly penning.

With the arrival of the waiter, our thoughts turned to food, the four of us opting to share a fish *meze*.

"*Ta psaria meze gia tessera*," I requested, prompting Bill to comment, "You've got the lingo down pat by the sound of it. It can't have been easy getting to grips with a new language at your age."

"Well, we didn't want to be the sort of expats who make no effort," Marigold said, a guilty look flitting over her features as she realised she'd rather let her formal Greek lessons lapse of late.

"I prefer the term European citizens with Greek residency," I added.

"Quite," Bill agreed. "It makes you wonder where the term expat originated. Do you suppose the first English fellow to live abroad was called Pat?"

"I think you'll find that it's short for expatriate, relating to someone who lives outside their native land."

"Fancy that."

"After exploring the ruined castle, we wandered round the old town of Itilo," Emily said.

"Wonderful little place," Bill added.

"Itilo dates back centuries, it's steeped in history. It even got a mention in the Iliad," I said.

"Oh, isn't that the latest Jeffrey Archer? I nearly picked that up at the airport, didn't I, Bill?"

"Homer was a bit before Archer's time," I pointed out, struggling to keep a straight face. "Itilo may appear as a sleepy backwater now but it was a thriving town a couple of centuries ago, renowned for piracy and slavery."

"Perhaps it was the slaves that carted all those stones up that great hill," Bill remarked.

"The thought of pirates is exciting," Emily gushed. Despite her obvious enthusiasm, her Botoxed face refused to express any emotion. For the first time I noticed that along with her frozen features, Emily's right eye looked more than a tad droopy, casting an oddly unsymmetrical aspect to her face.

"Such a charming little town. We wandered through the cobbled streets and stuck our heads in a couple of churches," Emily said.

"Then we stopped for a coffee at this little place..."

"We weren't sure whether to go in, it didn't look too inviting...we got some funny looks from a few old men sitting inside..." Emily interrupted.

"But we took the bull by the horns and sat down outside," Bill continued as though they were a well-oiled double act.

"We didn't order anything to eat..." Emily said.

"No need after that wonderful breakfast you knocked up...that cheesy egg thing you did was superb, Victor."

"But they brought us some food anyway..."

"It would have been rude to leave it...wouldn't it, Emily?"

"Little saucers of sliced cucumber with olives

and thick chunks of sausage speared on tooth-picks…" Emily said.

"And he refused to accept a cent for it…just charged me for the coffees. Sixty cents was all. I said to Emily, with prices like that, we could take a long weekend here and still have change from a tenner."

Chapter 15

The End of a Relationship

Although I had expected the luncheon date to be an excruciating ordeal, surprisingly I found myself enjoying the company. It crossed my mind that Bill and Emily may have been excellent company for our regular visits to the Bhilai Bhaji back in Manchester, but we had never really socialised with the neighbours there as we did in Meli. It gladdened my heart to see Marigold on top form: relaxed and revelling in the banter, she looked quite lovely teasing a Titian tress away from her forehead.

Relishing the picturesque surroundings and

appreciating Marigold's beauty, I barely registered when she insisted that Bill and Emily must return next year for our vow renewal celebration. Cringing at the extravagant way in which Marigold doled out invitations willy-nilly to every man and his dog, I bit my tongue. There was no point in ruining the atmosphere by taking her to task about turning the small celebration into a veritable circus. If it all got ridiculously out-of-hand expense wise, I would put my foot down and get Violet Burke to knock up some Spam sandwiches we could eat on the beach. I could turn on the charm and convince Marigold it was romantically retro.

With the arrival of the *meze*, the conversation waned as we focused on tucking into the delicious food. The taverna had excelled itself, producing a platter positively groaning with fried *kalamari* and two types of anchovies, marinated and deep fried. Grilled octopus nestled next to giant grilled prawns, with octopus in vinegar on one side. Olives, sliced cucumber and tomato wedges were dotted between the tasty marine offerings, with hunks of bread to be dipped in *tzatziki*. The *meze* was accompanied by a plate of chips so perfectly fried that even Violet Burke wouldn't have turned her nose up, though she would definitely have swerved the octopus.

"Couldn't imagine dining alfresco in Manchester

at this time of year," Bill observed. "I might be tempted to strip off and take a dip when we've finished lunch. Fancy joining me, Victor?"

"He'll have to give it a miss," Marigold answered for me. "I forgot to put our cossies in the car. I didn't expect it to be hot enough for an impromptu dip. It's certainly a treat to have glorious weather like this in December."

"There's always skinny dipping," Bill quipped.

"I don't think Neo Itilo is a designated nudist spot," I objected before Bill could get carried away.

"Look, there's someone in the water." Emily pointed towards a lone swimmer in the sea.

"I can't make anything out," Bill said.

"There, see that straw hat," Emily persisted.

"The Greeks often take to the sea in their hats," I explained as the four of us focused our attention on the hat bobbing around in the sea. After a few minutes, the figure emerged from the water, revealing itself as a rake thin elderly gent complete with straw sunhat.

"*Einai to nero kalo*?" I called over, asking him if the water was good.

"*Kalo,*" good, he confirmed, wrapping a towel around his waist and slowly picking his way across the pebble beach.

"He swim every the day, one half the hour, rain or shine," the waiter told us. "He say it keep him young."

The conversation between Marigold and Emily turned to their chance encounter during my wife's recent return to Manchester to visit Geraldine. Savouring an exquisitely marinated anchovy or *marinarismeni gavro* as it is known in Greek, their chatter washed over me. My thoughts turned to the events which Marigold had relayed to me following her visit.

After a succession of unsuitable boyfriends, leaving Barry maligning her as a man-mad harpy desperate for any random fellow to get down on one knee, Geraldine had turned up in Greece with the sexually infected Ashley in tow. Whilst initially besotted enough with Ashley to drag him along to Greece and inflict him on us, Geraldine had soon come to realise he was a crashing bore with an indecorous line of patter when it came to polite dinner party conversation. No one wants to have their noses rubbed in sexually transmitted infections while they eat, especially when the person doing the rubbings repeatedly refers to them as VD.

Following their somewhat romantic sojourn in Meli, the scales fell from Geraldine's eyes on her return to Manchester. As Ashley's thoughts turned to marriage, Geraldine thoughts became fixated on dumping her tedious nylon-haired suitor. Confiding in Marigold, Geraldine admitted that rather than being the prince charming she had dreamt of sweeping her off her feet, Ashley was just another in a long line of ill-matched frogs. After an evening in his company listening to him drone on about moulage, mould and venereal diseases, I had reached my own conclusion that Ashley was an insufferable bore.

Nevertheless, Geraldine's determination to ditch him had been hampered by Ashley's pathetic romantic history of being jilted at the altar. Geraldine, convinced Ashley would be left a broken man if she rejected his anticipated proposal, had turned to Marigold to come up with a cunning plan to turn the tables. Conspiring together, the two women came up with a way to make Geraldine appear so repugnant that Ashley would surely dump her: if their plan succeeded, Geraldine would be rid of him with a clear conscience.

Marigold had described an excruciating evening in the Bhilai Bhaji, an evening she had been looking forward to immensely as our son Benjamin would be joining her and Geraldine in our favourite Indian restaurant. Ashley, too thick-skinned to pick up on Marigold's hints that his presence wasn't wanted, confided in my wife that he intended to join them and propose marriage to Geraldine that very evening. Since Marigold had stood him up at Argos where she was meant to help him choose a suitable ring, he resorted to digging out the tarnished engagement ring that he had previously stuck on the finger of his first fiancée: she had happily thrown it back in his face at the altar, proclaiming the cheap nasty metal turned her finger green.

Duly forewarned of Ashley's intentions, Geraldine dressed for the occasion in the most slatternly get-up designed to repulse her prudish boyfriend. Pulling out all the stops in a tarty and age inappropriate outfit coupled with garish make up plastered on with a trowel, Geraldine bore a shocking likeness to the sort of past its sell-by-date slapper that hangs around plying their grubby trade in the rough streets beneath Piccadilly Station. As an aside, I must add that such details were according to Marigold: personally I have no experience of ageing prostitutes or their condom littered insanitary environs. Considering that Geraldine looked like a blowsy tart, according to Marigold, it is doubtful that she would have even been granted admittance to the Bhilai Bhaji were it not for the proprietor fondly remembering my wife.

Apparently Ashley was so wrapped up in recalling some tedious work triumph pertaining to a breakthrough in some sexually infected specimen curdling in a test tube that he failed to even notice Geraldine's bizarre appearance. Hogging the conversation, he droned on relentlessly, boring my wife and son to the limits of their endurance, his specialist subject of gonorrhoea putting them off their much anticipated dish of gobi matar. As an aside, I had warned Marigold to avoid any cauliflower dishes in Ashley's company, but she chose to ignore it.

Despite Geraldine's obvious efforts to control her heaving bosom which threatened to spill over her sequin top, Ashley was so engrossed in his test tube saga that he barely glanced at his beloved all evening. However, the moment the waiter served Geraldine's chicken jalfrezi, Ashley sprang into action, throwing himself down on one knee with no regard to any suspicious stains on the carpet. By that point Geraldine was completely sloshed, an understandable state considering she had spent the evening intercepting lecherous looks from every male in the restaurant with the exception of Ashley and Benjamin. Geraldine's glazed eyes narrowed to a squint: attempting to focus on the boring fool at her feet, she thrust a forkful of curry into her mouth. Ashley leant forward and grabbed her arm, imploring her, "Don't swallow it."

Washing down the forkful of curry with a slug of wine, Geraldine slurred, "It's not polite to spit food out on the table," before hiccupping loudly.

"You've just swallowed your engagement

ring," Ashley cried. "I thought it would be romantic to have the waiter hide it in your curry. I didn't think you'd be stupid enough to eat it."

Even inebriated, Geraldine didn't react well to Ashley's demand that she retrieve the ring from the toilet bowl when it passed through her digestive system: the very suggestion that it would be as good as new once she'd given it a good polish was enough to sober Geraldine up. Realising that the plan to thwart Ashley's proposal hadn't worked, Marigold stuck her two-penn'orth worth in by revealing to Geraldine that the ring would never be as good as new as it wasn't new in the first place, having previously graced the finger of Ashley's first fiancée. To make matters worse, Marigold, fearful that Geraldine might come down with a nasty case of blood poisoning from the cheap nasty ring contaminating her innards, suggested they should head to the hospital. It appears that my wife did pay attention on occasion when I lectured her on the dangers of insanitary foreign objects turning up unexpectedly in the food.

Until this point, Geraldine had been happy to provoke Ashley into dumping her rather than have him suffer a second jilting. Everything changed when Geraldine heard that Ashley had tried to palm her off with someone else's corroded ring. In the course of the subsequent embarrassing public row, Ashley got the huff and flounced out of the restaurant, not even bothering to settle his share of the bill. His glaring lack of good manners was the final straw as far as my wife was concerned and she lost no time in convincing Geraldine it was time to call time on Ashley and stuff the consequences. Marigold pointed out that if his wounded pride left him lacking the confidence to ever get close to another woman, then said woman would have a lucky escape.

Three days later Geraldine passed the ring: she didn't bother disinfecting it before returning it to Ashley with a curt note saying their relationship was over. The Bucket household is overjoyed to know that Ashley is gone like the clap after a good dose of penicillin and will never darken our door again.

My reflections were disturbed by my mobile ringing. Glancing at the screen, I saw the caller was Spiros. Mindful that I did not wish to appear boorishly rude by taking the call at the lunch table, I excused myself and stepped down to the pebble beach.

"*Ela*, Spiro," I greeted my friend.

"Victor, it is the Nikos…"

"Niko, how are you? Spiros said you were going to the hospital, what happened?"

"We to leave the hospital now, many hour we

to wait…the injury is the *tipota*," Nikos said, claiming it was nothing. Knowing Nikos, he would have considered it unmanly to make a fuss even if he'd spent the last few hours hooked up for a blood transfusion.

In the background I could hear Spiros berating Nikos for saying it was *tipota* before demanding the phone.

"*Ela*, Victor." I held the phone at a distance as Spiros practically blasted my ear off. "You have to work the grill tonight. The Nikos, he cannot to use the arm…"

"What on earth happened?" I interrupted.

"The Nikos to nearly lose the arm. The Guzim cut to the bone with the, how you say, the *prioni*?"

"With a saw." I barely held onto my lunch as a vivid image of a petrol fired chainsaw slicing through tender flesh flooded my brain.

"The doctor to say the Nikos is the lucky he not the one-arm bandit…"

"But they're sending him home."

"Yes, I to bring him home now. You must to work the tonight, the Nikos cannot to grill. The arm is kaput, the doctor to put him in the swing…"

"I think you mean sling," I corrected.

"And he cannot to see the grill…"

"What do you mean, he can't see the grill?"

"The Guzim nearly have the Nikos' eye out

with the stick. The doctor to put him on the patch…"

With his arm in a sling and a patch on one eye, it sounded as though Nikos was only missing a parrot perched on one shoulder to pass as a modern-day pirate. Before I could voice this thought, Spiros snapped me back to the present, insisting, "You must to work the grill tonight, Victor."

"Hold on a sec. Why is it my responsibility to take on the grill?" I protested.

"You expect the Dina to be in the two place at once? How she to cook the *patates* and *salata* and be outside at the grill? You have the to work in the taverna before, you must to help or the Nikos must to close." Spiros was adamant in his assertion as though the subject wasn't open for debate.

"I worked in the taverna kitchen, it's an entirely different kettle of fish," I pointed out.

"The Nikos not to grill the fish…"

The idiom had clearly gone over Spiros' head.

"I know nothing about working the grill," I said firmly. "I was never one for a Sunday barbecue."

"What is there to know? You just to throw the meat at it…"

"Well, if it's so easy, why don't you step into the breach and throw the meat at the grill?"

"People not to want the food cook by the undertaker. They to imagine where my hands have to been and it put them off the meat. The Nikos will to sit and explain you how to grill," Spiros argued in his most persuasive tone. The thought of Nikos sitting barking orders at me did nothing to enamour me to the prospect of skivvying in the taverna again.

The sound of Nikos shouting at Spiros in the background permeated the line and I heard Nikos yell, "Tell him the Dina think of him like the son."

"You cannot to let the Dina down, Victor. She think of you like the son, yes." Spiros dutifully parroted Nikos' words, seemingly unaware I had already heard the unsubtle coercion.

"Why can't Kostis stand in for his father?" I asked, mentally conjuring myself a get-out clause.

"The Kostis he off hunting. I am the sure he will to return to help out the father when he gets the breeze of what happen."

"Wind of, not breeze. It's when he gets wind of it..." I could feel my resolve to have nothing to do with the whole sorry business weakening as I considered the motherly Dina bravely soldiering on single-handed. "So, Nikos just needs me for tonight?"

"Yes, just the only tonight... and maybe the week or two...think of the Dina," Spiros wheedled.

"All right, tell him I'll be there tonight," I reluctantly relented. "But tell him that if he tries to guilt-trip me into doing his olives, I will down my pinny and tongs and walk out."

"The Nikos ask are you the any good at play the *bouzouki*? He cannot to play with the arm in the swing..."

Terminating the call, I wondered how Marigold would react to the news that I was about to resume cheffing at the taverna for the foreseeable. No doubt she would insist I strip off on the balcony in the cold night air when I returned home stinking of grilled chicken and pork.

Picking up a pebble, I skimmed it towards the sea. The water wasn't calm enough to register any ripples as the stone hit the surface, the waves crashing onto the beach in a swirl of white foam. Turning to re-join the others at the lunch table, I gawped in shock at the sight of a beached white whale bowling across the beach. It wasn't an actual whale of course, though Bill, stripped down to his tighty-whities with his pallid paunch on display, certainly resembled one. He cut a ludicrous figure. Whilst I am sure his intention was to run across the beach before launching his paunch in the water, his progress was more of the mincing variety, leaping up and down like a scalded cat as his feet came into contact with the sharp shingle. Finally reaching the water, he waded in up to his thighs before demonstrating a spectacular belly flop.

Returning to the table, I asked Emily, "You don't fancy joining him?"

"Best if I don't. I'm no good in the water without swimming goggles." Touching her face self-consciously, Emily blushed.

"I expect we have a pair in the boot you can use," I offered, toying with a piece of now cold *kalamari*. The squid had lost its appeal, the fried batter soggy and uninviting thanks to Spiros interrupting my lunch.

"No, you misunderstood. I don't like to go in the water without goggles unless it's calm. I hate getting salt water in my eyes but goggles aren't very advisable at the moment." I had no idea what Emily was on about. Noticing our perplexed expressions, she leant forward, whispering, "I had a treatment just before we left England and I've read horror stories of goggles leaving imprints."

"You've lost me," I said.

"Well, I know you'd never notice it if I didn't mention it…I've had Botox injections."

"Yes, Marigold said she thought you had…ouch." The 'ouch' was in response to my wife kicking my shin under the table.

"That was invigorating," Bill said, pulling his shirt on over his still sopping body and plonking his soaking backside down on a chair "So, Victor, what do you think? Do you fancy joining us?"

"Joining you where?"

"Didn't you tell him, Marigold? While you were off gabbing on the phone, I extended an invitation for you and your good lady wife to join us for the night in Sparta. We'll treat you to a hotel room and dinner, least we can do after your hospitality."

"It's a very generous offer," I said, thinking it was far more than we deserved after the atrocious welcome we'd given the couple the previous evening: after leaving them to their own devices to heat up Fray Bentos pies, we could hardly claim to be the most gracious of hosts. "But I'm afraid that we must decline...ouch."

The 'ouch' was in response to another sharp kick from Marigold.

"I think it sounds fun, Victor. A night away would do us good," Marigold cajoled, fluttering her eyelashes enticingly, apparently belatedly realising a seductive approach may reap more rewards than a sharp kick.

"I'm sure it would and I'd have been all for it if I didn't have to work this evening," I said.

"Work. You're practically unemployed at the moment apart from those cookery classes and you do those during the day," Marigold argued.

"Well, I have to work tonight. Nikos nearly lost his arm and has been at the hospital all day," I explained.

"Lost his arm," Marigold cried, the colour draining from her face.

"And an eye. Something to do with Guzim and a chainsaw. I don't have all the grisly details; suffice it to say that I've been headhunted to work the outside grill."

"Headhunted," Marigold scoffed.

"Okay, guilt-tripped into it. Spiros really laid it on how Dina can't manage to run the taverna on her own."

Taking my hand, Marigold's tone softened as she told Emily and Bill, "Dina can work Victor round her little finger; he's putty in her hands."

"And you don't mind another woman…" The shocked outrage in Emily's voice wasn't reflected on her frozen face.

"Oh no, it's not like." Marigold clutched her ribs, her tinkling laughter attracting the attention of the other table of diners. "Good grief, no, Victor isn't the type to go round attracting other women."

I coughed to signal my disagreement, thinking how quickly Marigold had forgotten the way that Sherry had thrown herself at my head.

"Dina's a sweet old thing. She thinks of Victor like a son. He helped her out in the taverna kitchen during our first winter here and they've had a special bond ever since," Marigold said.

"Dina's own son Kostis is a waste of space, forever off carousing and chasing women and hunting...even so, Dina treated him like the sun shone out of his backside..." I said.

"Well, at least until Eleni left him, taking Dina's darling baby granddaughter with her," Marigold added.

"I'm stepping in for Dina's sake but I will have to suffer Nikos barking orders at me all evening. I haven't got the first clue when it comes to grilling outside," I confessed.

"Bill can give you some tips. He likes nothing more than doing a good barbecue on a Sunday, don't you, Bill?"

Chapter 16

Surprised by a Peeping Tom

I t was late afternoon by the time we arrived home. Marigold, desperate to discover who Sherry had been frolicking in a field with earlier, announced she was off to call on the English woman to get the low-down: quite how my wife's mind turned a likely innocent stroll into a risqué liaison eluded me. Before leaving the house, Marigold disappeared to enjoy a rejuvenating shower. Whilst Marigold was engaged in the bathroom, I took advantage of the last of the daylight, stepping onto the balcony with a welcome cup of Earl Grey.

Sipping my aromatic cuppa in my favourite

spot, I watched the comings and goings of the villagers as they made their way home after a long day harvesting olives. I was surprised to see Dina doing a passable imitation of a pack donkey, carting a full sack of olives over one shoulder: Guzim, dragging a sack, trailed in her wake, his guttural complaints drifting up to the balcony. For once I could sympathise with the Albanian shed dweller: I had almost given myself a hernia attempting to haul one of Dimitris' sacks off an olive net, a full sack of olives weighing almost as much as my wife.

I relished the peace before the storm so to speak: my evenings would no longer be spent relaxing with a good book in front of a blazing log fire, but huddled over a grill belching smoke. Whilst I had quite enjoyed my previous stint cheffing at the taverna, I had been in the warmth of the kitchen with Dina clucking over me like a fond mother hen. Standing around outside in the bitter cold of a December evening, taking orders from Nikos, didn't hold quite the same appeal.

Relegated to a fixed spot outside, I would have little opportunity to practice my Greek with the regulars, though I expected I would be subjected to plenty of Greek expletives every time I opened the door to allow cold air and smoke inside the taverna: perhaps I should persuade Barry to come along and translate some of the more colourful profanities I could expect to be hurled in my direction. I suspected that the 'one night' or 'maybe a week' that Spiros had mentioned may well end up stretching out over several weeks if Nikos' injuries were as lurid as the undertaker painted them. If Dina needed me, and Kostis didn't ride to my rescue, I knew that I would end up being a pushover. Still, as Marigold had pointed out with a tad too much enthusiasm for my liking, it would spare me from being idle and keep me from getting under her feet: I rather imagined her keenness related to the latter point.

A piercing scream startled me from my reflections. The scream reverberated with alarm, a distinctly different timbre to the more usual hysterical yelps I associate with Marigold's regular encounters with some unusual Greek creepy-crawly. Dashing to Marigold's aid, I narrowly avoided dousing Clawsome with scalding tea before colliding with my frantic wife running out of the bedroom, her modesty protected with nothing more substantial than a flimsy hand towel.

"Phone the police, Victor. There's a peeping Tom at the bedroom window," Marigold screeched before slamming the bathroom door in my face.

"A peeping Tom," I repeated sceptically, presuming Marigold must be delusion: it would be a bit of a challenge for any voyeuristic pervert to letch over my near-naked wife since the bedroom window isn't on ground floor level and there are no conveniently placed trees for any random degenerates to climb.

Striding into the bedroom, I was shocked to come face-to-face with Violet Burke's Jehovah's Witness peering in at me through the window: the glass pressing against his face flattened and distorted his features, making his nose appear pug like. I was taken aback when he gave me a cheery wave, his mouth stretching into a tentative grin. It was hardly the sort of reception one would expect from a lecherous perve caught in the act of ogling one's wife. Perchance he was lurking at the window with more nefarious intentions.

Rather than confronting him at the window, I hot-footed it down to the garden hoping to cut him off before he could make his escape. It struck me that if he was intent on burglary, he was a tad indiscreet. If his penurious state had tempted him to branch out from unblocking random toilets into looting and pillaging the local houses, he may want to consider a career change. A savvier burglar would surely have borrowed Violet Burke's balaclava and waited until dark to creep around trespassing. A master criminal would surely have more nous than tapping on the window pane and waving at the householder he intended to rob.

"What on earth do you think you're doing?

Explain yourself at once," I shouted up to young Theo. Balanced on a ladder propped up against our bedroom window, he didn't appear in the least embarrassed to be caught in the act nor in any great hurry to make a getaway.

"Hello, Mr Bucket. Kyria Burke told me to clean your windows. She borrow me this ladder and told me there is much need for the person to clean windows." Droplets of cold water anointed my head as Theo waved a soggy sponge around.

"Flaming cheek. She might have asked me if I wanted my windows cleaned before she sent you up that ladder," I replied, noting that it was actually my ladder the young man was dangling from: I didn't recall my mother asking if she borrow it. Taking a deep breath, I realised that I had allowed my imagination to go into overdrive and that the Jehovah's Witness had nothing more diabolical in mind than making my windows shine.

Marching into my garden like a bolshie harridan on a mission, Violet Burke hollered up to Theo, "I hope you're putting some welly into it, lad."

"Welly? I not understand."

"It's a figurative term meaning to put some force into it," I explained.

"They're all smeared, lad. Anyone would think you'd never cleaned a window before. Hop down and I'll give you a demo on how to do them proper like," Violet Burke instructed.

"Is the beach clear?" Theo called down.

"Come again?" Violet Burke retorted. "You've no time to be thinking of gadding about on the beach, lad. You've a whole load of grimy windows to clean if you're going to make a living at it."

"I not want to wet you if the water spills from the bucket..."

"I think he's mixing up his idioms, Mother. I think he wants to know if the coast is clear before..."

"Aye, lad, I'm well clear of your bucket," Violet Burke interrupted me. Theo deftly slid down the ladder, his clumsy landing sending mucky water from his bucket spilling all over my slippers and soaking my socks.

Elbowing Theo aside, Violet Burke heaved her bulbous form onto the bottom rung.

"Mother, I really don't think it's wise for you to climb that ladder," I cautioned as the ladder began to wobble precariously under her weight.

"'Appen you're right, lad," she concurred. "Victor, you'd best get up the ladder and show young Theo here how it's done."

"What's the point of you telling him to clean my windows if you expect me to show him how to do it? If you've decided to employ a window cleaner, it would have made more sense to find an experienced one," I carped.

"I'm just trying to do the lad a good turn…there's no window cleaner in the village. I thought if he could turn his hand to it, he could have a good business going in no time at all." Turning to me, she looked me up and down before sniffing. "I'm surprised you didn't think of turning your hand to it yourself, Victor. You're practically unemployable. It won't do you any good to sit around idling or you'll find yourself turning into a vegetating tippler like that Norman fellow."

"It's a bit late in the day for me to think about launching a new career as a window cleaner," I retorted.

Although balancing up a ladder whilst wielding a shammy held not the slightest appeal, I reflected that age had been no barrier to my dabbling in new adventures in a new country. Since taking early retirement and relocating to Greece, I had turned my hand to cheffing in the taverna kitchen, repping during the holiday season and managing the village shop. On top of that I had earned some lucrative commissions from luring house buyers Spiros' way, conducted cookery classes and penned a book that could well turn into a runaway best seller. All in all, I considered, not too shabby a showing for practically unemployable.

Turning to Theo, Violet Burke sighed. "I should

have realised you're a novice, lad. 'Appen with all them wives you lot have, the menfolk leave the window cleaning to the women."

"Wives," Theo stuttered in confusion.

"Mother, I think you are confusing the Witnesses with the Mormons, the Jehovah's lot don't go in for polygamy."

"The Kingdom Hall did not have any windows, Kyria Burke, but I am willing to learn…"

"Never you worry about cleaning any halls, lad. You can practice on Victor's windows…"

"He's referring to his place of worship," I explained before wondering why I was bothering. "Look, Theo, I think my mother has come up with a good business idea for you but if you want to make a go of it, you'll need the proper tools for the job. A bucket of mucky water and a sponge that has seen better days just won't cut it."

"Proper tools?" my mother queried.

"Yes, proper tools. I would suggest he starts out with a heavy duty rectangular bucket that will accommodate a combo squeegee and window scrubber. He'll never fit an extendable squeegee into that round bucket," I said, recognising Theo's bucket as the one that lived under my kitchen sink. I supposed I should be grateful that my mother hadn't furnished him with my washing up bowl.

"You can't beat a bit of old newspaper, vinegar

and elbow grease," Violet Burke protested.

"Have you seen the price of newspapers, Mother?"

"Well, pay him for doing your windows and he can use the cash to get sorted with the right equipment to make him proper like," Violet Burke demanded. Glancing up at my newly smeared and streaky bedroom window, I thought the cheek of my mother knew no bounds. Still, her intentions were noble and it shouldn't take the eager young man long to get the hang of it once he was properly kitted out.

Doling out enough cash to get him started, I suggested, "Until you're tooled up, Theo, why don't you start out by giving my mother's windows a good cleaning? Since the *apothiki* is on street level, my mother can show you how it's done without either of you having to venture up a ladder."

"And you might as well lend the lad your ladder until he can afford to invest in one of his own. It's not as if you ever go up it…"

It was pointless arguing. The stubborn look on Violet Burke's face showed her mind was made up.

The bathroom window was flung open and Marigold stuck her head out, calling down, "Victor, are the police on their way? Is it safe for me to come out of the bathroom yet?"

I was instantly filled with guilt. I had completely

forgotten that Marigold had been scared half out of her wits by an unknown man popping up at the window whilst she was dressing.

Catching sight of Theo, Marigold shouted, "That's him. That's the peeping Tom."

"It's okay, darling," I reassured her. "He isn't a Peeping Tom. He's that young Jehovah's Witness I told you about..."

"The one that your mother has been encouraging?" Marigold huffed. "I've heard it all now. It was bad enough having that lot going door to door in Manchester but no one warned me that Greek Jehovah's went around proselytising through upstairs windows."

"He wasn't up there dishing out copies of the Watchtower: he was cleaning the windows," I explained.

"Since you're such a slattern when it comes to a mucky windowpane, I got you a proper window cleaner, lass."

Narrowing her eyes in anger at Violet Burke's insult, Marigold withdrew her head, slamming the window shut with such force that it would be a miracle if the glass survived. Still, it would be one less window for Theo to tackle.

"You'd think that wife of yours would be grateful I've gone and found her a professional window cleaner," Violet Burke complained. "Victor, I'm expecting you to put the word about so young Theo can land himself lots of clients. Now, I haven't got all day to be hanging around; let's get on with my windows sharpish, there's a mountain of spuds waiting for me at the taverna that won't peel themselves."

"I'll be working there myself later. Nikos has had an accident and needs me to man the grill…"

"If you're going near that grill of his, I'd better take my Vim along and give it a good scouring, Victor." I winced at my mother's mention of Vim, imagining the usually flavoursome meat transformed into something inedible, seasoned with gritty cleaning powder. There was always the possibility that if I served up Vim flavoured meat, Nikos may sack me. "It would turn your stomach if you saw the state of all that congealed fat and gunk he's let build up. It's a breeding ground for germs…hang on, did you say he's had an accident? Poor fella. He must be near death's door if he's letting you near that filthy grill of his…he's right particular who goes near it."

"The hospital have patched him up and sent him home. I'll be grilling under his supervision…"

"I'm glad to hear he'll still be around. He's not so bad as bosses go even if he does have some strange foreign habits…'appen I'll take him some home-made biscuits to cheer him up."

"That's very thoughtful of you, Mother."

"Aye well, the kitchen is fair bursting with them. Random Greek women keep knocking on my door to give me the things. They won't take no for an answer. I can't be doing, they're so sweet they make your teeth scream and so dry they take hours to chew: kourab something or other they call them..."

"They sound like *kouranbiethes*, mother. They're very popular," I said, attempting to hide my surprise that our Greek neighbours were plying Violet Burke with local delicacies.

"Now them honey dumpling things what Maria does are more my cup of tea..."

"*Loukoumades*," I said, my mouth salivating at the thought. The hunger pangs kicked in, a reminder that Spiros' phone call had disturbed my lunch. Thinking that the sooner I could get shot of my mother and her young charge, the sooner I could rustle up a snack to tide me over, I ushered the pair of them out of my garden.

Leaving Theo to manhandle the hefty ladder, I trailed behind him carrying his bucket, almost colliding with Marigold as she hurried down the outside stairs.

"I'm off to call on Sherry. I hope she likes home-made biscuits," Marigold said, waving the packet of *Gemista* chocolate biscuits that I had bought from the shop that morning. I reflected that my wife seems to have the most extraordinary knack of convincing herself that anything shop bought that she tries to pass off as home-made really has been in actual contact with our oven.

"Oh look, there's Norman heading our way. See what he wants, Victor. I don't want to get caught listening to him banging on about traffic cones."

Chapter 17

A French Fancy Bribe

A h, Victor, the very man," Norman greeted me, his obsequious expression hinting he was after something.

"I'm afraid that if you're in need of cooking tips, now's not a very good time," I pre-empted him, hoping to make a clean getaway.

"No, nothing like that. I brought a batch of my latest French fancies over for you to sample," Norman said, extending a large Tupperware box. There was no misinterpreting his gesture as an obvious bribe when he added, "I was hoping I could persuade you to lend me your ladder and give me a hand hanging my Christmas decorations. Did I mention I'm doing up the outside of the house with traffic cones draped in lights?"

"It's barely December, Norman," I objected, wondering if he really thought I was such a cheap date that he could buy me with a few French fancies. His sweet offering didn't even appeal, fondant having a tendency to stick in my teeth.

"I know," Norman sighed. "Ideally, I would have liked to have them up from the beginning of the month but I only collected my new extension cables from the post office this morning."

"Well, I'm afraid you're out of luck, Norman. I haven't got time, plus I've just said that Theo here can borrow my ladder for his new window cleaning round."

"'Appen you could pay young Theo here to give you a hand stringing up your decorations," my mother interrupted. Turning to her young charge, she urged, "Get round there with the ladder sharpish, lad, and give Norman a hand hanging his Christmas lights. I bet you're a dab hand at that even if you know nowt about shining windows proper."

"I wouldn't bank on it, Mother," I said. Not wishing to embarrass the young man, I added in a whisper, "Jehovah's Witnesses don't celebrate Christmas. They consider it a Pagan festival."

"Don't do Christmas. There's nowt pagan about it. The Blossoms were Methodist but still did it," Violet Burke declared, not bothering to lower her voice.

"Witnesses don't celebrate it as they believe there is no proof that Jesus was born on Christmas day. They don't celebrate birthdays either," I said.

"My church teaches such celebrations are sinful," Theo clarified, doubt discernible in his voice. He was clearly waging a personal battle, questioning the convictions drummed into him during childhood.

"Sounds a bit bloody miserable," my mother scoffed. "Fancy not being allowed to have a decent knees-up on your birthday."

I bit my tongue to prevent myself blurting out something I would prefer Norman not to hear. Until I had been reunited with my absconded mother two years earlier, I had been clueless to my actual date of birth, thus depriving me of almost sixty years of birthday celebrations. Although Violet Burke had pencilled the exceedingly unfortunate name of Victor Donald on the piece of cardboard safety-pinned to the pink frilly bonnet she had tied on my head when she abandoned me in a bucket, she had neglected to add the momentous date on which I had been delivered in the back of the chippy.

Insensitive to my decades of lost birthdays, Violet Burke announced, "I'll be wanting a proper shindig for my eightieth next year."

Hearing her words, my anger dissipated: surviving eighty years of hard graft and grinding poverty amid a sea of greasy chip fat was certainly worthy of a celebration. Marigold would surely be onboard if I suggested throwing Violet Burke a party to mark the occasion.

"I like to see a good display of Christmas lights. We used to hang a flashing crab up at the chippy…"

"A crab doesn't sound very Christmassy," Norman said.

"Well, it was the nearest thing we could get to a flashing haddock," Violet Burke snapped. "I think lights are right festive after all them years of blackouts. Mind you, I was quite partial to a bit of darkness when I had to make do with drawing gravy lines on the backs of my legs…"

"Gravy lines?" Norman was clearly confused, unfamiliar with my mother's convoluted ramblings.

"It wasn't easy getting your hands on a pair of nylons during the war." Violet Burke rolled her eyes at Norman's naiveté. "Still, Victor's father made sure I always had plenty of soap to wash off the gravy…"

"I think you should give Norman a hand to

hang up his traffic cones, Theo," I interrupted before my mother could divulge any details about the limping soap salesman who had spawned me. It wouldn't do to have my personal life the subject of expat gossip. "If it won't compromise your religious principles, of course."

Sensing the opportunity to have his traffic cones illuminated, Norman cajoled Theo, "I'll see you right cash wise and you can sample some of my latest baking." Lifting the lid from the Tupperware box, he showed off his French fancies. I couldn't believe it: he'd only gone and shaped them into traffic cones, using orange fondant decorated with butter cream for the white lines and chocolate for the finishing touch of a neatly piped 'No Parking.'

The prospect of cake appeared enticing enough for Theo to risk Armageddon. Hoisting my ladder onto his shoulder, he took off after Norman.

Finally free of the budding patisserie chef, the inept window cleaner and my infuriating mother, my grumbling stomach reminded me that I needed to eat before my shift in the taverna. Relieved to have the house to myself, I heated up some home-made *avgolemono* soup. Alas, I barely had time to skim the surface of the tasty lemon and chicken broth with my spoon before the peace that had descended on the Bucket household was rudely disturbed by

Milton barging in.

"I say, old chap, I need your help. There's a bit of a crisis, what."

"What is it now, Milton?" Only a tone-deaf dunce would fail to pick up the hint from my long-suffering tone that his intrusion was unwelcome.

"There's some Greek woman going ballistic at ours, appears to be threatening Edna but we can't make head or tail of anything she says. Edna kept trying to tell her to speak English but she just keeps ranting on in Greek. Really could do with your help, old chap, see what it's all about," he pleaded pathetically.

"Don't you think that it's about time that you mastered some Greek, Milton? I can't be at your beck and call every time you have some petty disagreement with one of the neighbours." I made no attempt to disguise my impatience.

"Doubt that she's a neighbour, old chap. Never clapped eyes on the woman before," Milton argued.

"That still doesn't detract from my point. If you could understand her, you wouldn't need to drag me out," I grumbled, reluctantly grabbing my jacket and scarf. Casting a wistful glance at my soup, I determined to introduce Milton to the concept of over-stepping neighbourly boundaries.

The light was fading fast as we approached Milton's place, my ears assaulted by the strident sound of raised voices.

"Do you think I should rope Norman in to help? Solidarity in numbers and all that, what," Milton asked, pointing in the direction of Norman's house. Through the gloom, I could just discern our fellow expat passing a traffic cone up to Theo. The young Witness perched unsteadily on my ladder struggled to maintain his balance, weighed down with enough extension cables to power Battersea Power Station.

"Fat lot of use Norman would be, his Greek is as dismal as yours," I responded.

Reaching Milton's house, I didn't recognise the elegantly dressed middle-aged woman with smartly coiffured hair as a local. In full flow, she barely paused for breath as she berated the cowering Edna, my English neighbour feebly protesting, "If you could just tell me in English. I don't understand Greek. Speak English."

It struck me that the Hancocks were a lost cause. There was no excuse for their failure to at least memorise the stock phrase for 'I don't understand Greek,' *den katalavaino Ellinika*. Said with a smile, it would at least show willing and make them come across as less pig-ignorant.

"*Kalispera Kyria. Poio einai to provlima?*" Greeting the Greek woman, I asked what the problem was before telling her I would translate. "*Tha metafraso*."

Stabbing a finger in Edna's direction, the woman accused, "*Afti i gynaika echei klepsei ti gata*."

"She says that you have stolen her cat," I told Edna.

"*Otan epestrepsa sto spiti mou sto Meli apo tin Athina, i gata mou eleipe*," the Greek woman continued.

"She says that when she returned to her house in Meli from Athens, her cat was missing," I added.

"*To eida ston kipo tis gynaikas. Otan tis eipa na to dosei piso, to evale sto spiti*."

"She says she saw her cat in your garden but when she told you to give it back, you put it inside the house."

"I put all the cats inside when she started shouting, I didn't want the poor things getting upset," Edna defended. "Cats are sensitive creatures."

"Edna, do you have her cat?" I demanded.

A touch of defiance crept into Edna's voice when she acknowledged, "I might have."

"You can't just go around stealing any cat that takes your fancy," I pointed out. To be frank, I was surprised by Edna's recalcitrant attitude. It was one thing to go around the village hoovering up strays to give them a home: it was quite another matter to deliberately kidnap a pet with an owner, though catnap may be a more appropriate term.

"It wasn't like that. The cat has been hanging around for weeks now, getting thinner by the day and looking ever more bedraggled. He was clearly too domesticated to cope with scavenging in the bins." Firing a look of disgust at the Greek woman, Edna continued, "Do you know that there are Greeks who have holiday houses here but live in Athens? When they go back to the city they turf their cats onto the street and leave them to fend for themselves until they can be bothered to come back. It's cruel. Maybe I took her cat in to give it a proper home."

"Even if that's the case, Edna, you can't just go around snatching other people's cats. There are laws against that kind of thing."

"I didn't snatch it. I adopted if off the street," Edna insisted. "She neglected it."

"You can't go around hurling wild accusations. First of all, let's make sure it is her cat. I will ask her what it looks like," I reasoned. "*Pos moiazei i gata sas?*"

"*Einai kafe me krema koilla.*" The Greek lady sounded calmer as she furnished me with the cat's description.

"She says it is brown with a cream belly…"

It was evident from Edna's expression that she was familiar with the cat.

"*An den to epistrepsei amesos, tha kaleso tin*

astynomia." The woman's voice took on a threatening tone.

"She says if you don't give it back immediately, she will call the police."

"And I will tell them that she abandoned her cat and they should arrest her for animal cruelty," Edna retorted.

"And exactly how are you going to tell them that when you can't speak Greek? You can't expect the police to speak English for your convenience. Just hand the cat over, Edna," I demanded, having no intention of hanging around to translate if the police turned up. My encounters with the local constabulary were becoming a tad too regular for my liking.

"Best do what Victor says," Milton advised his wife. Shuffling nervously, he looked decidedly shifty as he added, "Wouldn't do to invite trouble with foreign police, what."

As Edna reluctantly went indoors to retrieve the Greek woman's cat, I hollered across to Norman, "Do me a favour, Norman, and fetch that box of French fancies over here."

Whilst we waited for Edna to emerge with the cat and for Norman to arrive bearing cakes, I made small talk with the Greek lady, not only discovering that her house in Meli had been in her family for four generations but that Athena was her second cousin. Since Athena is *nona* to my niece, Anastasia, I supposed that made us very loosely related in the Greek sense.

"I'm glad I could tempt you with my fancies, Victor. You know how much I value your culinary opinion," Norman panted as he landed at my side firmly clasping his Tupperware box of goodies.

"They're not for me, Norman. Let's just say I intend to use them to improve diplomatic relations in the village," I told him, presenting his box of iced offerings to the Greek woman.

Lifting the lid, she stared suspiciously at the iced cakes. *"Efcharisto, eimai sigouros oti i gata tha ta apolafsie to keik."*

Snatching the cat back from a reluctant Edna, she stalked off, a firm grip on the wriggling feline and the cake box.

"What did she say?" Edna asked sniffily.

"She said she was sure the cat will enjoy the cake."

Chapter 18

Some Other Poor Sap

Delighted to have averted a neighbourly conflict from escalating into a full blown Maniot feud of epic proportions, I strolled home at a leisurely pace, my thoughts turning to Violet Burke's eightieth birthday the following year. The villagers loved any excuse for a celebration and amazingly my mother had managed to make a few friends amongst the local Greeks. In spite of their inability to communicate in any meaningful way, Violet Burke had been accepted warts and all by a small coterie of admittedly eccentric types. Moreover, she was already becoming indispensable to the local expats, though I suspect that a few of them simply tolerated her because they are too bone-idle to do their own cleaning.

I pondered the likelihood of any of my mother's old beaus still being alive and kicking, wondering how she would react if they descended on Meli for a birthday bash. It struck me that I still had a few gaping holes in my knowledge about my mother's past. Whilst she had never been reticent about disclosing her amorous encounters during the war, I still had a gap as far as her marital history was concerned. I was painfully well informed about Violet Burke's first husband's atrophied testicles and her third husband's philandering ways in the back of the Odeon that resulted in triplets. I was well up on her fourth husband's bigamous exploits before he met an untimely end, flattened under the wheels of the number 47 bus, yet not a single word pertaining to husband number two had ever passed my mother's lips. I decided to take the opportunity to tackle her about it later, perchance whilst she was tackling Nikos' mucky grill with the Vim.

"*Kalispera*, Victor. You come in for the coffee?" Dimitris' invitation startled me, bringing me back to the present. The light had faded and I had almost passed Dimitris' door without noticing his presence.

"*Alli fora, Dimitri*," I replied, saying another

time. "I have to check on the chickens and then I must head off to the taverna. I'm taking over for Nikos at the grill..."

"Ah, yes. I hear you will be cooking the meat. We must all pull together in this difficult time for Nikos…"

Pausing mid-sentence, Dimitris took the time to drag a hard backed chair from inside to the doorstep. It didn't surprise me that news of Nikos' accident was already the talk of the village.

"Some of us are being pulled rather more than others." Waving the offer of a seat away, I raised an eyebrow sardonically at Dimitris' suggestion that we were all in this together; I didn't see him being roped into skivvying. Dimitris' idea of support most likely amounted to reluctantly stopping by the taverna and hastily guzzling a plateful of grilled chicken before scuttling away hurriedly in case Nikos persuaded me to have a go with the *bouzouki*.

"You will be cooking the meat and I have volunteered to help with Nikos' olive harvest. It is too much for Dina to manage alone with only the cretinous Albanian to help."

Whilst instantly overcome with shame at my egotistical presumption that I was the only one lending a helping hand, I couldn't help but be impressed by Dimitris' apt usage of cretinous. His mastery of English was coming along in leaps and bounds thanks to our regular language sessions.

"It will not be easy to work the Nikos' olive alongside the Kyrios Stavropoulos..." Droplets of sweat erupted on Dimitris' forehead in spite of the drop in temperature. Wiping them away with his sleeve, there was a frantic edge to his jerky movements.

"Surely he's a bit past it to be doing the olives," I exclaimed, picturing the cantankerous pensioner whiling away his mornings downing sweet coffee outside the shop whilst perusing a dog-eared copy of *Rizospastis*, the daily newspaper put out by the Communist Party.

"He offered to help too." Dimitris visibly shuddered as he spoke. His obvious discomfort made me recall that there was no love lost between the two men: in fact, Kyrios Stavropoulos was capable of starting a Maniot feud of his own. I had personally witnessed the grouchy old-timer openly deriding the learned professor as a traitor to *Kommounistiko Komma Elladas*, the Communist Party of Greece. He delighted in targeting Dimitris with continual barbs about his habit of wearing his long hair tied back in a ponytail, deliberately tormenting the younger man by clacking his *komboloi*, or worry beads, in a passable imitation of a popular Communist ditty. Gory visions of the pensioner threatening my friend with dangerous olive picking implements flooded my mind. With any luck, the old man's bad back would render him incapable of wielding anything more menacing than a non-mechanised olive comb.

"There will be many the hands to the trees. The old men who drink coffee with the Kyrios Stav-ropoulos say they to help Dina too. Tina say she will open the shop late to give the hour with the trees and Sampaguita will help if she can spare the time from caring for Giannis' grandfather."

I hoped the calming presence of the level-headed Filipina would prevent any geriatric fisti-cuffs amongst the olive groves.

"It's too much work for Dina, she's in her sev-enties yet still expected to run the taverna kitchen every evening," I said. "Are you familiar with the idiom many hands make light work?"

"Yes, it is similar to the all hands to the deck-chairs…"

I was relieved to hear so many villagers with time on their hands were willing to muck in. Each volunteer reduced the risk that Nikos would make it his mission to have me toiling over his olives all day before donning my chef's hat in the evening.

As though reading my mind, Dimitris said, "Nikos have much to say about how he hope that you would help with his olives. But I tell him you are the…how to say in English…the neither use or trinket?"

"It's neither use nor ornament," I corrected coldly, bristling at his offensive words. Really, I had given the ungrateful wretch the best part of a morning picking his olives to only belatedly hear that my efforts were not only unappreciated but reviled.

"You not to have the knack..." Dimitris took one look at my affronted expression before changing tack. Flustered, his carefully cultivated English suffered a serious setback. "I mean to the say, you has no the olives in your Manchester, England. How you can be the experienced with no the experience? The olive he take the lifetime to learn."

"It's not easy keeping one's balance on a three-legged ladder, not to mention those sacks of olives were dastardly heavy," I agreed, my anger diminishing as I recalled Nikos telling me that Dimitris was nothing more than an amateur when it came to olives: most likely the learned professor didn't have a clue when it came to gauging my competence. "I expect it would take you a while to get to terms with cultivating rhubarb."

"What is the rhubarb? I think I hear the word before..."

"A vegetable I dabbled with in my Manchester garden."

Slapping a fist against his forehead, Dimitris exclaimed in Greek that he remembered the word,

"*Thymamai ti lexi.*" Reverting to English, he continued, "The Violet Burke to put the rhubarbs in the crumble. Now I am the confuse: I think the crumble he is the sweet dessert."

"Rhubarb's an odd one. Technically it's a vegetable but when it's doused in sugar it is often served up in sweet pies and puddings," I explained.

"I think you eat the bizarre foods in the Manchester…"

"Wait till my mother gets started on spotted dick and jam roly-poly. Speaking of strange things, have you been seeing much of Sherry?"

"Sherry?" Dimitris stammered, his English faltering again as he continued, "That woman to frighten the jeebie-heevie out of me…"

"It's the heebie-jeebies, Dimitri, but that was an excellent stab at a popular English idiom."

Appearing more concerned with expressing his feelings than accepting praise for his progress in English, Dimitris brushed off my compliment. "She is the man hungry. How you to say, what is the word…*poia einai i lexi*?"

"*Apelpismenos*, desperate," I suggested in both our languages.

"Desperate, the Sherry she is the desperate. She remind me of the *mavri arachni chiras* who spin the web to catch the prey."

Amused by Dimitris' analogy to Sherry as a

black widow spider, I confirmed, "So, you haven't been seeing her?"

"Not if I to see her coming. It is not the manly to hide but I admit to the hiding. She unnerve me more than the Kyrios Stavropoulos."

"Well, I wouldn't be too worried. Marigold's convinced she has some other poor sap in tow."

"The poor devil. Rather him than me," Dimitris replied in excellent English.

Chapter 19

A Quaint English Tradition

C losing the front door on the world, I stretched languidly, releasing the kinks from being pulled in every direction by the demands of my hapless expat neighbours. The prospect of a window of peace before leaving for my cheffing stint offered a welcome opportunity to recharge my batteries. My quietude was short-lived when Marigold called out from the bedroom, her tone quiveringly nervous, "Is that you, dear?"

"Sorry, I didn't know you were back from Sherry's. I didn't mean to startle you," I called back, chastising myself for not realising my wife was likely to be feeling a tad jumpy after her earlier encounter with a strange man popping up at the bedroom window. Even though Theo was harmless, Marigold was bound to be disconcerted by his out of the ordinary appearance.

As she joined me in the kitchen, I couldn't help but notice something seemed a bit off. Marigold appeared preoccupied; fidgety and casting anxious glances behind her.

"Where did you get to?" she asked.

"Just over to Milton's. Edna has been going around stealing cats..."

"That's nice, dear."

Clearly my wife was paying as much attention to my words as she does when I lecture her on the importance of sponge hygiene.

"You might feign some interest, dear. I said Edna's been snatching cats off the street...I suppose it's a good thing that your coddled domestics never venture outside. No risk of them being catnapped," I quipped. "What on earth is my bowl of *avgolemono* doing on the floor?"

"Silly me, I must have confused it with cat food." Swooping down, Marigold scooped up the bowl, tipping the contents down the sink. I sighed in frustration at the waste. Since both Clawsome and Catastrophe demonstrate a marked aversion to anything with lemon, I had planned to reheat the soup, confident it would have been spared a good licking from the cats.

"Never mind. I will make do with some bread and olives," I said resignedly.

"Sherry wasn't at home so I left a note inviting her and 'her friend' to join me for dinner in the taverna." Gesturing with air quotes as she voiced the words 'her friend,' a pretentious habit I particularly deplore, Marigold indicated she thought there was more than friendship going on. "I've asked Barry along too, I don't want to look like a spare part if Sherry doesn't turn up. Since you're going to be there anyway, I thought I might as well come along and keep you company whilst you play at barbecuing."

"I won't be playing," I bridled, doubtful that Marigold would shift from her cosy seat by the wood burner to venture outside to keep me company whilst I toiled over the grill. Still, at least Barry would be on hand to give me a crash course on the choice Greek expletives I anticipated the customers hurling in my direction. His presence would be a stroke of luck since I was rather relying on him to give me a few pointers on lighting the grill. I wasn't a hundred percent convinced that my idea of chucking some firelighters on the charcoal was the best way to start it. Kerosene flavoured meat might not go down too well with the regulars, even if I smothered it in oregano.

Spearing an olive straight from the jar with a toothpick, I noted, "These olives are excellent. Where did they come from?"

"Litsa. She gave them to Barry but he isn't keen unless they're pickled in vinegar."

"She does spoil your brother, they're awfully good. I just had a word with Dimitris and he's definitely not walking out with Sherry. He freely admitted she frightens the pants off him."

"He ought to grow a backbone. She's just a bit full-on but she means well. I was pretty sure it was Dimitris that she's been sneaking around with."

"You shouldn't rush to judgment. There may be no sneaking around involved. It's probably all above board and she just hasn't got round to introducing this mystery man to her circle yet."

"All above board, what piffle. Well, at least according to your mother: she says it's all very cloak and dagger. Vi reckons Sherry won't want it coming out that she's bought herself a kept man."

"You shouldn't put too much stock in the things my mother comes out with," I advised.

"Well, your mother is right about Sherry seeing someone on the quiet. I definitely saw her slinking off into a field with a man earlier and she's never mentioned a new boyfriend. If it isn't Dimitris, then I can't think who it could be. He had long hair but I didn't get a look at his face." Marigold was like a dog with a bone.

"So she hasn't splashed her cash on a haircut for him. I can't think of any other long haired local men apart from Dimitris. Perhaps her new man isn't from around here. She's always on the lookout for expat groups to crash; perhaps she's found true love with a Brit."

There was a definite trend for the village men to sport similar hairstyles because most of them tended to frequent the local barber, Apostolos, known for his signature short back and sides with a lopsided neckline. Even Spiros no longer bothered splurging the extra on a decent haircut from a barber in town: revelling in domestic bliss with Sampaguita, he had no need to impress the ladies and had given up on his habit of making *kamaki* with tourist women. Naturally I hadn't let my own standards slip, taking whatever evasive action was necessary to avoid Apostolos getting within scissor happy range of my head.

"Well, your mother is convinced that Sherry is spending her money on a man. It's desperately sad the lengths some women will go to…"

"Surely that's no surprise to you. Geraldine epitomises desperation. Look at how many lemons she's squeezed over the years…"

"She's sworn off men after Ashley. She's taken

up yoga instead…"

"She'll soon get bored of that. Geraldine doesn't strike me as the type to have enough patience to find inner peace by navel gazing…"

"You do come out with the oddest things, Victor. I don't think it's possible to get a good view of one's navel while attempting the downward-facing dog…"

The sound of whimpering distracted Marigold, her train of thought lost.

"What's that? It sounded like there's a dog in the house," I said.

"Don't be ridiculous, Victor. It was just one of the cats. I put them in the spare bedroom so they wouldn't shed hairs on your mother's newly mopped kitchen floor."

"I didn't know she'd been in with her mop today…"

"Well, she hasn't, but if I keep the cats out then the floor will retain that newly mopped look for longer."

To my ears, Marigold's reasoning sounded pathetic at best, not to mention her reddening cheeks hinted she was fobbing me off with some lame half-baked truth. In the name of marital harmony, I decided to make allowances: no doubt she was still suffering the after effects of shock from being caught in a state of dishabille by a religiously lapsed

Jehovah's Witness.

"Speaking of my mother…"

"I didn't realise we were…"

"Did you know that she hits the milestone of her eightieth birthday next year? I was thinking we ought to throw her a party. Nothing too extravagant, just a select gathering of her friends and any old beaus I can dig up."

"Don't you think select is bit of an oxymoron where your mother is concerned?"

"I was using select in the sense of not a free-for-all," I clarified, having a suspicion that dodgy, brash and vulgar would be a more apt description than refined when it came to Violet Burke's known associates. "We could surprise her by having a few of her friends over from England."

"What? And put them up here? Are you out of your mind, Victor? I have no intention of turning my home into a doss house for rejects from Saga Holidays. Anyway, Vi may want to go back to Warrington next year."

"It's not looking likely now she's taken on so many cleaning jobs. She won't want to let people down, not with her work ethic…"

"Frankly, your mother mixes with the types I'd rather not give houseroom too."

"Well, she gets on like a house on fire with your new best chum Moira and Sampaguita is very fond of her."

"I had other undesirables in mind."

"Such as?"

"Well, there's Maria from next door for a start, you know I prefer to give her a wide berth, she's awfully hard to get rid of once she gets her foot in the door...and then there's your drunken chum Vasos..."

"I thought you liked the good *Kapetainos*."

"Well, I do. He has a certain charm in small doses but that's not to say I want him cluttering up the grand salon when he's half-cut. He's not exactly a good influence..."

"At eighty, I think my mother is past being influenced..."

"Your mother is a lost cause, Victor. I was referring to you. I never did get to the bottom of that business about you spending a night carousing in his company when I was in Manchester. I've heard a few hints that it was all a bit debauched. Don't think I haven't noticed how you get terribly close-lipped whenever I press you about it."

In truth, I had only the sketchiest of memories where that particular night was concerned. Crossing my fingers behind my back, I protested, "It was just an innocent night out with Vasos and Vi. I was hardly likely to get up to mischief with my geriatric mother in tow. Anyway, if you don't want to throw her a party at home, we could hold the celebration in the taverna."

"If we hold it in the taverna the place will end up swamped with gate-crashers. We'd never live it down if your mother made an exhibition of herself in front of half the village. Not to mention that it would hardly be the definition of a select gathering," Marigold argued.

"We could invite Douglas over. For some inexplicable reason the twins seemed quite fond of my mother. You know how much you'd love to see Elaine and the girls again," I wheedled.

"We'll see them when they come over for our vow renewal service."

I was surprised that Marigold was so against the idea of throwing my mother a party, her vociferous objections only beginning to make sense when she peevishly added, "It's a pity you can't show as much enthusiasm for our vow renewal service as you do for throwing your mother a shindig."

"It's hardly the same thing. My mother will only turn eighty once whilst we've been happily married for nearly four decades. Since we are both true to the vows we exchanged on our wedding day, I don't see the point of going through the whole rigmarole of repeating them again…" I stopped mid-sentence, the ideal solution flashing into my mind in a Eureka moment. "I've got it. We can hold a joint celebration: combine renewing our vows with Violet Burke's eightieth."

I realised my suggestion had gone down like a lead balloon when Marigold fired a withering look in my direction before practically spitting, "I wonder if Spiros has the name of a good divorce lawyer."

From down on the street, the distinctive sound of grinding brakes and the crunch of metal clunking against metal broke through the tension in the kitchen. Before we had time to react, a cacophony of blasting car horns broke out. I hadn't heard such a din in Meli since the car procession arrived back in the village following Barry's wedding.

"What on earth?" Rushing across the room, I threw the French windows open and stepped out onto the balcony, Marigold close behind me. At first glance it appeared a line of cars and vans was stalled bumper to bumper, queuing into the distance. Leaning over the railings for a better view, I noted a couple of bumpers were slightly more intimately entangled than I had gauged from my initial assessment. Against the backdrop of incessant hooting, Vangelis threw his van door open. Jumping out, he strode to the back of the van, clearly prepared to lay into whatever moron had driven into the back of him. Amidst his slew of expletives, I caught *tyflos ilithos*, blind driver, before Vangelis' words froze on his lips, his mouth gaping open in shock when he realised the driver he was cursing was none other than his own wife, Athena.

"*Agapi mou. Eisai pligomeni*?" Vangelis cried out, meaning, 'My love. Are you hurt?'

"*Ochi, alla to aftokinito einai,*" Athena replied that she wasn't hurt but the car was, before asking her husband why he had braked so suddenly, "*Giati frenarises toso xafnika?*"

It seemed that although Athena had driven into the back of her husband's van, that wasn't the reason for the hold-up: the vehicles in front of Vangelis' van had all ground to a standstill too, concertinaing into one another like a row of out of control dodgems.

"What's going on?" I shouted down, recognising Barry step out of Cynthia's old banger, caught in the traffic jam a couple of vehicles ahead of Vangelis.

"I can't see from here, it looks like it started further ahead. Cynthia's going to be hopping mad when she sees this prang in her bonnet."

"By the look of things, you've rear-ended Panos' tractor," I shouted down.

"With a bit of luck, he'll never notice. It was hardly in pristine condition to start with," Barry called up. "I'll just wander along a bit and find out what the problem is up ahead."

"I've never seen traffic jammed up like this before," I said, ushering Marigold back into the warmth, curious to hear what Barry would discover.

Clearly distracted, Marigold murmured, "That's nice, dear," her ears visibly twitching as the sound of scratching emanated from the direction of the guest bedroom.

"What's that peculiar noise?" I asked.

"I told you, it's the cats." Marigold visibly reddened when the scraping sound turned into a whimper.

"The cats don't whimper like that..."

"Perhaps we've got mice..."

Marigold was clearly attempting to keep something from me. The mere mention of mice is usually enough to send her scrambling onto the kitchen table in a state of hysteria.

"The sonic devices deter mice. What's going on Marigold?"

My wife was saved by the bell, or to be more exact, her brother hollering up from the street. Moving back out on the balcony for an update on Barry's traffic report, I warned Marigold, "I intend to get to the bottom of whatever funny business is afoot as soon as I've spoken with Barry."

"You've never seen the like, Victor. It's full-on bedlam, Greek style. Come down and see for yourself," Barry called up. "This pile-up goes right round the bend…don't worry, no one's hurt, but they're making a right song and dance about the state of their bumpers and you wouldn't believe what caused such chaos."

"I'll be right down. Are you coming, Marigold?"

"I'll give it a miss. It's a bit chilly out there." Her answer surprised me. It is not like my wife to willingly miss out on something with gossip potential.

As soon as I reached the street, Barry grabbed my arm, practically dragging me along amongst the jostling villagers flooding out of their houses to get a good gawp. Everyone seemed determined to get a first-hand look at whatever was causing such excitement, pushing and shoving in their eagerness. Rounding the bend in the road leading to the village square, cries of "*Ti einai afto*?" meaning 'What is it?' echoed in the night air.

Edging my way past the line-up of cars snarled bumper-to-bumper, my worst nightmare came true when I caught sight of the tacky illuminations clearly responsible for distracting the drivers and causing the vehicles to collide into each other. A giant traffic cone fashioned in a poor imitation of Santa stood in pride of place, serving as a major distraction for any approaching traffic. Despite being kitted out in the traditional red stocking cap complete with pompom and what looked suspiciously like a fondant beard, the decked out cone bore more of a resemblance to a plastic traffic warden than Father Christmas.

The shoddy imitation Santa was prominently positioned in front of a whole slew of traffic cones swathed in flashing multi-coloured 100watt light bulbs surrounding the perimeter of Norman's house, spewing onto the narrow pavement by the side of the road. Rather than appearing festive, the overly-bright gaudy display resembled the warning lights put out to alert vehicles to slow down as they approached the site of a major road accident. Naturally such a display had encouraged the drivers to slam their brakes on without first consulting their rear view mirrors, too eager to rubberneck in the hope of catching sight of something morbid to pay any attention to road safety.

"I don't believe it. Norman and his blasted flashing traffic cones. He needs his head examining," I spat. "How could he be so brain-dead? Surely he realised that he's set his stupid decorations up to look like there's been a major accident, though in Norman's case he's been the one to cause it."

"It didn't bring that to mind until you mentioned it, Victor," Barry mused. "My first thought was road works. Those lights remind me of the sort of set-up you see when there's a big hole being dug in the road or a bit of off-side tarmacking. Still, you've got to admit he's done a grand job with that Rudolph on his roof. Anastasia will love it."

"What Rudolph?" I'd been so mesmerised by the streetside display inviting vehicular carnage that I hadn't even noticed the inflatable reindeer on Norman's roof, its vinyl antlers encased in twin-kling fairy lights.

Norman sidled up next to us, his chest puffed up in pride. "What do you think, pretty impressive? There are some rather unique ones. They might all look similar to the uneducated eye but I've got a fair mix between rubber, flexible polymer and bog standard plastic finished off with reflecting tape."

"I can't tell them apart," Barry said.

"You've clearly got an uneducated eye, Barry. Just look at the way all these cars have stopped to take a good gander at my conic selection," Norman boasted, misinterpreting the mayhem he had caused as fascination in the visual display of his hobby.

"I think you've lost your marbles…"

Although Norman had droned on endlessly about his traffic cone collection, boring me rigid through many an expat dinner party, I'd never re-ally paid any attention to his trite monologues about hunting down unique channelizing devices and pylons. Now that the things were illuminated in all their glory, all I could see was a mass of orange and white stripes with no discernible differences between the conical safety markers.

"See that one on the pavement; it's one of the original concrete ones. And that blue one by the door came all the way from Japan," Norman droned on, completely oblivious.

"You blithering idiot. These drivers didn't stop to admire them. They slammed on their brakes resulting in a mass rear-ending because they thought your Christmas display was a warning about a major accident..." I shouted.

"Or road works," Barry added. "Oh, look, here's Panos. I hope he's not going to kick up a fuss about the back of his tractor."

"Good Morning, Victor. You are looking very beautiful today," Panos greeted me in painfully slow English.

"What's with Panos? Has he developed a crush on you?" Barry asked.

"I'll fill you in later," I promised.

"*Giati yparchoun tosa polla fota se aftes tis odikes ergaseis?*" Panos said, asking why there were so many lights on the road works.

"*Den yparchoun odopoiies. Afta einai ta Christougenniatika fota tou Norman.*" My reply to Panos was eagerly listened to by a group of villagers closing in around me as I told him that there were no road works, explaining these were Norman's Christmas decorations.

"*Den einai Christougenna.*" Panos pragmatically pointed out that it wasn't Christmas.

Tina, having rushed out of the shop to see what was happening, piped up, "*Ta Christougenna den einai mechri ta teli Dekemvriou,*" pointing out that Christmas wasn't until the end of December. My last couple of winters in Meli had demonstrated that Christmas was a one-day wonder, not dragged out for weeks on end as it was back in England.

Panos momentarily confused me when he said he didn't see any boats, "*Den vlepo skafi,*" a sentiment echoed by the others. Their remarks began to make sense when I recalled that although gaudy displays of Christmas lights are not common in Greece, the Greeks do hang tasteful displays of lights in the shape of small boats. The previous year I had admired the charming twinkling lights lining the beach road in town and I had spotted similar festive displays strung up around small harbours.

"*Einai ena periergo Anglika ethimo gia na diakosmisete konous kykloforias ta Christougenna.*" Telling a bald-faced lie, I assured the curious Greeks that it is a quaint English custom to decorate traffic cones at Christmas.

Scratching his head, Panos stared at me long

and hard before doubling over with laughter. *"Panta ixera oti oi Angloi gavgizontan treloi."*

"What's he saying?" Barry asked.

"He said he always knew the English were barking mad."

"Trela Anglika." Panos' cronies took up the cry of 'Mad English.' I could only hope that as a European citizen with Greek residency, the Meli villagers didn't lump me in with Norman as a barking Brit. Moments like this prompted me to consider applying to become a Greek citizen and renounce my British passport.

My ears pricked up at the wail of a siren approaching.

"Sounds like the police are on their way to clear the road," Barry stated the obvious.

"Well, I have no intention of sticking around to be implicated in this mess," I said. "Norman, you are on your own. I am washing my hands of you. Good luck explaining your festive display to the police. I expect they will take your cones away as an exhibit if they decide to press charges."

"Don't you think you should hang around to give Norman a hand translating?" Barry objected.

"No. I'm sick of being exploited for my translating skills. Let him try his hand bribing the police with his fondant French fancies," I shot back.

Stalking off, I narrowly avoided colliding with

BUCKET TO GREECE (VOL.10)

Violet Burke weaving between the piled up vehicles on her borrowed bicycle, her cry of "It's not very Christmassy," somewhat muffled by her balaclava.

Chapter 20

Guzim Rabbits On

"There you are, darling." Marigold greeted me with a tender kiss when I arrived home. Considerately rushing to relieve me of my jacket, she urged me to take a seat by the newly lit fire and thaw out.

Resisting her enthusiastic attempts to divest me of my layers, I reminded her, "I still need to check on the chickens. I'll do it now before I sit down and get warm."

"Let Guzim see to them," Marigold protested, yanking my neck in an imitation of the hangman's noose in her eagerness to unwind my scarf.

"There's no point in you keeping Guzim if you insist on wearing yourself out by doing everything yourself. Now, do sit down and tell me what's happening out there. I'm all ears, dear."

Marigold's solicitous behaviour struck me as decidedly out of character, particularly in light of her earlier indifference.

"Norman and his blasted flashing traffic cones caused all the mayhem down there. Imagine trying to explain to a bunch of Greeks that illuminated traffic cones are a quaint English tradition. They're familiar with bedecked Christmas trees and displays of twinkling boats, but expecting them to fall for a load of old gumph about Christmas traffic cones being normal takes the biscuit."

"Personally, I can't see Christmas cones catching on but I'm sure your language skills impressed them no end. You do have a persuasive line in baloney, darling." Marigold's flattery alerted my being buttered-up detector, sending it into overdrive. At any moment I expected her to confess that she'd taken my credit card on an unauthorised spending spree around the frock department of Marks and Spencer. I made a note to check the back of her neckline later for any dangling tell-tale tags.

"Anyway, I got out of there before the police arrived. I refuse to hold Norman's hand…"

"Well, if he goes and gets himself arrested, at

least it will give Doreen a break. He's forever getting under her feet in the kitchen since he started your cookery classes. Do sit down, darling. I've been warming your slippers by the fire." The way Marigold was fluttering her eyelashes at me put me in mind of a deranged harpy. Although something seemed definitely off, it was quite a novelty to have my wife ministering to my every need with such devotion.

My good mood evaporated when I spotted visible teeth marks imprinted in the heel of one of my suede slippers, the other one shedding its sheepskin lining in fluffy abandon. "What on earth has happened to my slippers?"

"Umm, perhaps one of the cats was playing with them," Marigold stammered, the lie tripping easily from her lips as she'd seemingly forgotten her claim to have banished the cats to the spare bedroom.

"Or perchance those imaginary mice you were rabbiting on about earlier got hold of them." Tossing the slippers aside in annoyance, I jacketed up ready to flounce down to the garden to check on the chickens. The way she was acting, I would likely get more sense from Guzim than I would from my wife.

"I'd come down with you to check on your brood, but the cats have made a bit of a mess in the spare bedroom that needs cleaning up."

BUCKET TO GREECE (VOL.10)

Heading outside, I considered Marigold's stated concern for my clutch sounded fake to my ears: the only time she expressed any interest in my livestock was when she fancied bunging one of them in the oven for a Sunday roast. In addition to checking on the chickens, I was keen to shine some light on my winter veggies which had recently displayed evidence of some kind of pest infestation. I suspected that slugs or cabbage loopers may be making free with my cauliflowers, though I hadn't ruled out the possibility that Guzim's pet rabbit might be the nibbling culprit.

It struck me as a convenient coincidence that the moment I shone my torch on the cauliflower patch, Guzim appeared out of nowhere, cradling Doruntina in his arms. Perchance he had heard my approach, frantically snatching up his rabbit before I could catch it in the act of despoiling my caulis.

"Echei kouneli sou troie ta lachanika mou?" Dispensing with the usual pleasantries, I asked Guzim if his rabbit had been eating my vegetables. Whilst I have no objection to my gardener helping himself to the veg and sharing it with his pet, I found the idea of the creature gnawing away at some green stuff that may later end up on my plate befouled with rabbit spit, quite disgusting. Ever since mentally associating cauliflower dishes with the curdled contents of one of Ashley's test tube samples, I

have given the cruciferous veggie a miss. However, this winter's crop was coming along so nicely that I determined to overcome my aversion. I was keen to try out a new Greek recipe for braised cauliflower with cinnamon and tomatoes, *kounoupidi kapama*, preferably without the addition of some nasty zoonotic disease such as pasteurellosis or mycobacteriosis spread by the rabbit.

"*I Doruntina den itan pouthena konta sta lachanika sas.*" Adopting an aggrieved tone, Guzim claimed that Doruntina hadn't been anywhere near my veggies. Thrusting the rabbit under my nose, he demanded I look at her, saying she wasn't feeling well, "*Koita. Den aisthanetai kala.*"

I couldn't imagine why Guzim would be under the deluded impression that I should be able to detect if his pet was feeling a tad under the weather by simply gawping at the thing. My speciality is grubby kitchens, not rabbits.

"*I Doruntina ekana sex chthes gia proti fora kai tin afise travmatismeni,*" Guzim wailed, exposing his toothless gums.

Not believing my ears, I asked Guzim to repeat his statement that Doruntina had sex yesterday for the first time and it had left her traumatised. Since I would prefer not to litter the page with the crude terms Guzim used when describing how one of Giannis' rabbits had deflowered his precious

Doruntina, I will summarise our conversation, editing out Guzim's vulgarities and our use of Greek.

Although Guzim blamed himself for Doruntina's distressing experience, I was relieved that he hadn't personally done the deed: it would be unconscionable to retain the services of a gardener with an unnatural interest in bestiality. I do believe it is all above board and innocent when Guzim spends his nights cuddled up with furry companion.

According to the Albanian, his rabbit had been demonstrating signs of getting broody by rubbing her chin up against the back of Guzim's leg. Quite how he determined that chin rubbing was a sign that his pet was ready to mate was lost in translation: I think a bit of guttural Albanian may have got mixed in with his Greek when Guzim got technical. My observation that perchance his rabbit had merely had an itch to scratch resulted in Guzim citing his wife's expertise in these matters, Luljeta being an authority on rabbits since she scrapes a living by breeding the things on their dirt farm in Albania.

Guzim approached the honeyed and handsome Giannis, suggesting one of his colony might take a shine to Doruntina and be willing to do the dirty deed. At this point I interrupted Guzim's rambling tale to voice my concerns that if his rabbit fell pregnant, my garden may well end up infested with the things. Whilst a colony would not present a threat to my clutch of chickens, a mass presence of bunnies didn't bode well for my cauliflower florets. It struck me that if Doruntina started breeding like a rabbit, excuse the pathetic pun, the garden would soon be overrun.

Guzim confirmed my worries, informing me that it was common for rabbits to drop up to twelve kittens at a time. I must confess to thinking the Albanian shed dweller was losing his marbles when he started twittering on about his rabbit having kittens. My little quip that perchance he had mistakenly bred his pet with one of Giannis' cats went right over Guzim's head, confirming my theory that the Albanian shed dweller is sorely lacking a sense of humour. Whilst I endeavour to keep up-to-date with the sort of nasty diseases different species can carry and cross-pollinate to humans, there isn't much call for health inspectors to have an in-depth knowledge of their breeding habits or to be up on the fact that rabbits give birth to kittens.

Voicing my concerns about a potential influx of twelve new rabbits in my garden, I was relieved when Guzim said Giannis would keep all but a couple of kittens in part exchange for allowing the buck to use the doe as target practice for its insemination skills. Guzim assured me that he wouldn't allow any of Doruntina's offspring that he kept hold of to have free rein in my garden: he intended to keep them in the stone shed. They would serve as working contributors for his side-line of flogging manure: being odourless, there is a growing demand for rabbit poo for flower cultivation. I was surprised when Guzim mentioned that he already had Cynthia lined up as a customer: apparently she was keen on making the switch from pungent goat droppings. Moreover, after witnessing Doruntina's trauma, he had no intention of subjecting any of her kittens to the breeding process.

Recounting the traumatic events of the previous evening, Guzim told me that he had taken his rabbit along to Giannis' place, willingly allowing Giannis to put his delicate darling doe inside the buck's cage. I can't say that it came as too much of a surprise to hear that Guzim kept his eye on the proceedings rather than giving the mating pair some privacy. The buck duly followed the time-honed mating game of circling Doruntina, flaunting his tail like a regular stud as he checked the female out. Things then took an outrageous turn when the buck decided to spend a penny on Doruntina, sending her into shock. Although Giannis tried to convince Guzim that treating one's partner as a toilet splashback is perfectly normal rabbit foreplay, it offended the Albanian's sensibilities. Since I had never credited Guzim with having any sensibilities to be offended, I could barely prevent an enormous snort from escaping.

Sensing I was somewhat amused, Guzim climbed on his high-horse, telling me it was no laughing matter and lecturing me on the importance he placed on maintaining feminine hygiene standards for the doe: unbelievably he admitted to using baby wipes for regular wipe downs and combing her fur before bedtime. Considering that Guzim has a permanent blind spot when it comes to his own personal hygiene, I was easily amused when he became enraged that another rabbit had used Doruntina as a toilet. It was all too ridiculous for words.

Dramatic gesticulations, hair-pulling and much wringing of hands punctuated Guzim's gripes about the decidedly unromantic deflowering of Doruntina. He recounted that before he could rescue his pet from the coarse brute who considered water sports to be an essential part of the courting ritual, the doe had mounted Doruntina, and was having its wicked way: twenty seconds of honking later, it was all over with, the buck collapsing on its side as though waiting for someone to pass it a post-coital cigarette. Guzim claimed Doruntina hadn't enjoyed the experience at all and had been off her food ever since.

Retrieving his soggy rabbit, Guzim lectured

Giannis on the buck's unsuitability as a father figure to any kittens that may result from the encounter. I must confess to feeling a spot of empathy at
this point: I have always deplored the fact that Cynthia's vile mutant cat fathered Tesco and Pickles. I
made a half-hearted attempt to console Guzim, saying if Doruntina ended up pregnant from the encounter then at least there would be no need to subject to her a repeat performance.

For some inexplicable reason, Guzim started
spouting on about kindling. His change of topic
made no sense until he managed to mime that kindling is the word used to describe a rabbit giving
birth. I won't attempt to describe his mime since the
sight of the scrawny Albanian pretending to emu-
late a rabbit giving birth was truly indescribable. By
that point I was so sick of listening to Guzim rabbiting on about nesting boxes that I was sorely
tempted to make off with Doruntina and slap it on
Nikos' grill as that evening's special.

Eager to make my escape, I suggested to Guzim
that since Doruntina was feeling off-colour, he
should perhaps settle her down for the night in his
shed. Casting a nervous glance in the direction of
his slum dwelling, Guzim told me wanted nothing
more than to settle Doruntina down in his bed for
the night, but the rabbit was frightened of the dog
that Mrs Bucket had put in his shed. Before I had a

chance to react, Guzim prostrated himself on the ground, grovelling and pulling on my trouser legs, proclaiming he never intended those words to slip out.

"What dog? I demanded to know.

"Dog. I know nothing about a dog." Guzim's face was a picture of guilt as he repeated, "I know nothing about a dog; I am from Albania."

"I know you're from Albania, Guzim. It's hardly news."

"Your wife told me if you find out about the dog, I must say, "I know nothing, I am from Albania."

Clearly Marigold had been watching too many repeats of 'Fawlty Towers,' though that didn't explain what she was doing putting a dog in the shed. The last time a canine had been shut in the shed, it didn't end well.

My attempt to make my way towards Guzim's humble abode was somewhat impeded by the grovelling Albanian keeping a firm hold on my trousers. My attempts to shake myself free proved futile and I ended up dragging Guzim along face-down in my wake. Nearing the shed, I discerned the sound of whimpering from within. Kicking myself free from Guzim, I flung the shed door open to reveal Waffles chewing its way through a pair of the Albanian's underpants.

Grabbing the goldendoodle by the collar, I dragged it out of the shed and ran slap-bang into Marigold. No doubt she had been keeping a watchful eye on proceedings from upstairs and dashed down to the garden when she saw me heading for the shed.

"Marigold, what is the Stranges' dog doing in Guzim's shed?"

"Is it visiting with Guzim?" Her attempt to answer my question with a question didn't work.

"Marigold, Guzim told me you put the dog in there. What is going on?"

In spite of not understanding English, it must have been clear to Guzim that the Buckets were engaged in a domestic. Swivelling his head frantically between the two of us, he cried out, "*I Kyria Kouva me plirose gia na krypso to skyli sto spiti mou*," declaring that Mrs Bucket had paid him to hide the dog in his house.

Even as I allowed the full meaning of his words to sink in, I couldn't help but be amused at the way Guzim described the slum shed abode as his house. It really was touching the way he took such pride in being the owner of a scruffy stone shed on a postage stamped size piece of my garden.

"I can explain, Victor," Marigold said.

"I suppose you've taken a leaf out of Edna's book but instead of going around kidnapping cats, you opted to kidnap canines."

"I didn't kidnap the mutt. I'm doing Moira a favour. The taxi driver that took the Stranges up to the bus station refused to let the dog in his cab; it was having a bout of flatulence and the driver said he'd just had his Mercedes cleaned. Poor Moira was at her wit's end so I said that we'd dog-sit for the night."

"And you didn't think to mention it earlier? I suppose that explains what my *avgolemono* was doing on the floor. You were feeding it to the flatulent dog." Uttering the words, I offered a silent prayer of thanks that Marigold had tipped the soup down the drain rather than allow me to eat something the dog's drooling tongue had been dipping into.

"It was only flatulent because you insisted on feeding it stale oregano crisps and Norman's stew. Anyway, I was going to tell you that we were keeping Waffles overnight but thought it best to hide it in the spare bedroom until I could gauge your mood…"

"Where it promptly chewed up my slippers…."

"You weren't in the best of tempers when you got home from Milton's. When you popped out to check on Norman's lights, I took the opportunity to ask Guzim to keep an eye on it until I could find the right moment to break the news that Waffles will be staying with us overnight."

BUCKET TO GREECE (VOL.10)

"You mean bribed the poor sap to take it in and keep quiet. Not your shrewdest move, Marigold. Surely you realised Guzim is too dim to keep his mouth shut and your attempts to butter me up were completely transparent."

Our bickering was interrupted by a plaintive plea from Guzim, begging us to take the dog away so he could settle the traumatised rabbit inside.

"Did he just say his rabbit is traumatised? What happened to it?" Marigold said.

"Believe me, you don't want to know," I assured her. Even though I was cross with my wife, I wasn't feeling sadistic enough to inflict a dose of Guzim's rabbiting on her. "I suppose that since you have agreed to look after Waffles, we are stuck with it. Just keep it well away from anything of mine that looks chewable and don't let it get near the chickens. I'm off to work."

As I made to flounce off, Waffles nuzzled up against me, staring up at me with big wide eyes and wagging its tail. It was impossible to resist its appeal. I found it strangely ironic that after all Marigold's attempts to butter me up, it was Waffles himself that won me over.

Chapter 21

A Strange Case of Droopy

As is often the case after an exceptionally hot winter's day, the temperature up in our mountain village had plummeted to positively frigid by the time night set in. Smacking my gloved hands together to encourage the blood flow and ward off chilblains, I stepped into the taverna, taken aback that its typical image of a spit and sawdust establishment was a tad more polished than usual, showing evidence of a thorough bottoming. The fresh tang of pine cleaner infused with overtones of bleach filled the air, the burnt orange ceiling visibly free of its usual mosquito clogged and smoke-blackened cobwebs: clearly, my mother hadn't skimped on the scrubbing, making a thorough job of mopping the ceiling.

Dina and Violet Burke were sprawled in front of the *somba* with a large plateful of *kouranbiethes* my mother had taken along courtesy of her Greek neighbours. Ignoring the biscuits, they munched on bread, Dina dipping hers into olive oil, a thick layer of lard anointing my mother's hunk. Dina appeared aghast at the presence of the packet of lard my mother had smuggled over in her suitcase and plonked on the table. Melting in the heat from the wood burner, thick white sludge seeped from the paper, looking revoltingly unappetising. It went a long way to explain why the locals were so reluctant to sample foreign food.

Seated together in the still customer free taverna, the two women's inability to communicate in the same language seemed to be no barrier to their apparent easy companionship. I recalled that initially they had not taken to each other, my mother's overbearing bolshie manner provoking the ever placid Dina into putting her guard up. Icy conditions between them had thawed when Dina demonstrated her fondness for Benjamin, her treasured grandson being the chink in Violet Burke's armour. Since Dina loathed slopping the mop around and took a very lackadaisical approach to hygiene, she was grateful for my mother's undoubted superiority in that area, relieving Dina of the most loathed chore of her daily grind.

"*Ela kai kathiste,*" Dina welcomed me, patting a chair and telling me to come and take a seat.

When I asked how Nikos was doing, Dina launched into an account of his injuries and the doctor's prognosis. Even though she grumbled that Nikos made a terrible patient, concern for her husband's condition was etched on her gentle face. I attributed the defeated look in her eyes to a combination of weariness and worry. Dabbing the rheumy tears from her cheeks with a tea-towel, she brushed off my question about how Nikos' injuries had come about, telling me her husband would fill me in on all the gory details himself when he came down later to oversee my grilling. Apparently he was only willing to follow the doctor's orders to rest whilst the taverna was closed: his reluctance to linger upstairs once the doors were thrown open for business was understandable in a way. Nikos' larger-than-life personality ensures he is undoubtedly the main attraction of the place, adding that elusive something to the atmosphere that every taverna needs to make it a draw. I doubted even Dina's magnificent chips would be a big enough enticement if Nikos' presence was lacking.

Reluctantly rising from her seat with a sigh,

Dina opened the *somba* and chucked a log inside, asking me if I wanted a tot of *tsipouro* to warm me up. *"Thelete ena synolo tsipouro na sas zestathei?"*

"Ochi efcharisto. Den thelo na methynomai gia to kreas." Declining the offer, I told Dina I didn't want to be drunk in charge of the meat. I imagined that getting to grips with the barbecue would surely be a risky business involving hot coals and naked flames, especially dangerous if the wind picked up.

"What's she saying?" Violet Burke demanded.

"She asked me if I'd like some *tsipouro*…"

"I hope you told her where to shove it. Nikos makes his own, it's most likely pure poison. I don't want it giving you an episode like it did with your Great Uncle Bert."

"I have a Great Uncle Bert?" I shouldn't really be surprised: ever since reuniting with my mother, I had become accustomed to strange relatives crawling out of the woodwork.

"Not anymore, you don't, lad. He croaked it back when I was working in the munitions factory. Not that anyone noticed he was a goner…"

"He disappeared off the radar. What was it, missing in action?"

"No, he passed in his chair by the fire but no one noticed until he started whiffing a bit. He was never one to move much like, on account of his paralysis."

My mind boggled. I must confess to knowing little about Violet Burke's early years growing up in the bosom of the Blossom household, having only picked up the odd snippet here and there. Whilst my mother was forever dredging up stories from her past, they usually focused on events that had occurred after her family disowned her for bringing shame on the Blossoms by falling pregnant with me.

"*Ti leei?*" Dina asked what my mother was saying.

"*Mou leei gia enan palio theio,*" I replied, saying she was telling me about an old uncle.

"*Oloi eichame polla apo ta palia chronia otan oloi eichan megales oikogeneis.*"

"What's she saying?" my mother asked.

"We all had lots of them in the old days back when everyone had big families."

"Lots of what?"

"Uncles, I suppose." As an abandoned in a bucket orphan, I had been a tad short of uncles and other assorted relatives until of late.

Adjusting her headscarf, Dina ruffled my hair fondly, announcing she was going to pop upstairs and check on Nikos. Before heading for the back stairs, she squared her shoulders and slapped on a brave face.

"So, this Great Uncle Bert that I'm only now

hearing about, was he a Blossom?" I asked my mother, curious which branch of the family tree he belonged to.

"Nay, lad, he was nowt so grand as a Blossom, he was the last of them Smiths from a few doors down. The family took him in when he couldn't fend for himself on account of his droopy…"

"I think you mean dropsy…"

"Nay, we called his paralysis droopy on account of one side of his face hanging all…it's hard to describe it…"

"Droopy?"

"Aye, that's it lad."

"So he wasn't actually any relation to me at all…"

"Well, I suppose not. We had the habit in them days of calling everyone uncle, it wasn't considered polite to be so free with folks Christian names like you youngsters these days."

I reflected that if I was reading my mother's account correctly, the Blossoms had demonstrated compassion by taking in a partially paralysed neighbour in his hour of need, yet the same family had no compunction about chucking my mother out when she was caught out being a tad loose and free with her sexual favours.

"Course he brought the droopy on himself with that prison hooch he made when he was banged up;

toilet wine they used to call it. I could never make sense of it back when I was a lass. Every time Bert dragged himself off to the outside lavvy, I used to think he was popping out for a crafty tipple. He couldn't be open about his fondness for a nip, not after being given house room by a bunch of self-righteous, religious teetotallers."

"Prison hooch?"

"Aye, I felt a bit daft when I found out he'd not really been supping out of the toilet bowl. Even in prison, Bert couldn't stay free of the booze. He saved up his mouldy bread ration and used his socks as an illicit still. It was throwing a rancid potato into the mix that did for him, it give him a nasty bout of botulism. On top of his creeping paralysis, he was always coming over weak and dizzy: not that you could tell the difference, he'd never done an honest day's work in his life. By the time he got out of prison, he'd got that much botulism toxin in his system that the army could have launched him as a biochemical weapon."

Recalling Emily's propensity for Botox injections, I shuddered at the thought of her wilfully injecting such dangerous toxins into her system. If she wasn't careful, her immobile face may end up permanently paralysed, mirroring great uncle Bert's droopy.

"Before he got too bad to shift from his chair, he

used to use the tin bath to brew his bathtub gin while my mother was out at work. She didn't half kick up a stink when she found out what he'd been up to: being Methodist, she had no truck with having alcohol in the house. She was all for chucking him out until she discovered his home hooch was unparalleled when it came to bathtub cleaners: knocked the stuffing out of Vim it did when it came to shifting the greasy tidemarks my father left in the bath after a day at the factory. She'd have happily abandoned her principles and bottled that bathtub gin shine if my father hadn't been so big in the local Temperance Society."

"Well, I don't imagine that Nikos' *tsipouro* is quite as lethal as dodgy prison hooch," I laughed.

"I don't know, lad. It didn't agree with you the other week and that stuff you had was out of a proper bottle what came from a shop."

"What are you on about, Mother?"

"You were on the *tsipouro* when we had that night out with Vasos and his chum, what's his name? The one who never has much to say for himself."

"Sami. He doesn't have much to say for himself, as you put it, because he's a mute."

"He never said. I suppose that explains a lot. And what was the name of his girlfriend, she comes from some foreign place I never heard of?"

"Moldova…"

"Nay, lad, her name didn't start with an M. It was a right odd name, that I do remember. Something like horrible, let me think; Nastya, that's it. Nasty Nastya I called her, she might have taken the hump about that but she didn't understand a word of English. Don't you remember her? 'Appen you were too busy dancing with Maria."

"Maria?" My mind drew a blank. I had absolutely no recollection of hitting any dance floors with any Marias. Even after indulging in a few glasses of wine at special celebrations, I take Marigold's advice that it is better all-round if my two left feet sit out the dancing.

"Maria from next door. She nearly had that mute's eye out the way she was flinging her arms about trying to get the hang of the Hokey Cokey."

Before my mother could elaborate further, to my great relief Dina returned, sparing me from hearing anymore of Violet Burke's no doubt hyperbolic account of that still elusive evening. I would never live it down if Marigold got wind of me tripping the light fantastic with our elderly yet sprightly neighbour.

Whilst Dina busied herself making coffee, a bizarre three-way conversation of sorts took place, my head feeling like a shuttlecock batted back and forth between the two women as they lobbed their demands to know, "What's she saying?" and "*Ti leei?*" relentlessly in my direction. Dina informed me that Nikos' injuries had left him bad-tempered and he was going to be hell to live with until his sling came off. Despite doctor's orders to take it easy, he intended to take to the olive groves to supervise the harvest in much the same way he intended to oversee my grilling.

Without any warning, Dina emitted a piercing cry, dropping the *briki* full of bubbling coffee on the floor. Rushing to her side, my pulse raced in panic: I was convinced she was having a heart attack. Grasping hold of Dina's arm to prevent her from falling, I was shocked when she shook me off and ran to the door. As the door was thrust open, Dina threw her hands in the air, crying out, "*Einai thavma. Oi prosefches mou echoun apantithei.*"

"What's she saying," my mother demanded.

"I'm not that well up on religious Greek, Mother, but I'm pretty sure she said, 'It's a miracle, my prayers have been answered.'"

Dina's words made sense when a second later a young woman and a toddler appeared in the doorway, the pair of them immediately swept up in Dina's embrace.

"*Eleni mou. Nikoleta, glyko mou paidi, i koukla mou,*" Dina gushed, showering sweet words on her daughter-in-law and granddaughter and soaking the pair with her tears. Dina's face was transformed with joy into a picture of radiance, instantly dispelling the lines of fatigue weighing her down before their arrival. Pulling Eleni inside, Dina sank into a chair, cuddling Nikoleta tightly on her lap, proclaiming her happiness that they had returned between kisses.

"That's a sight for sore eyes," my mother observed, dabbing a stray tear from her cheek with her voluminous handkerchief.

"It's certainly a turn up for the books," I replied, feeling a tad emotional myself.

"I'll do the kiddie a nice plate of chips," Vi said, making her way to the kitchen.

"*Victor, boreis na to pistepseis? I Eleni kai i Nikoleta mou epestrepsan sto spiti*," Dina said, asking me if I could believe it, Eleni and Nikoleta had come home.

"Hello, Mr Bucket. I was so worried..." Eleni alternated between speaking in Greek and English as she explained to me that Spiros had telephoned her to say that her father-in-law was languishing on his deathbed following a near-fatal accident and had begged her to come home to look after her grief stricken mother-in-law. "It was so frightening to receive a call from the undertaker. I came at once, knowing my *pethera* would need me."

It struck me that Nikos had almost certainly been the one to put Spiros up to phoning his daughter-in-law, no doubt egging him on to deliberately exaggerate his condition in order to tug on Eleni's heartstrings to lure her home to Dina. I couldn't help but wonder how Eleni would react when Nikos miraculously rose from his deathbed, brandishing nothing more fatal than an arm in a sling and an eye patch. It would break Dina's heart if Eleni saw through Nikos' manipulation and upped and left.

Thinking it would be best to prepare Eleni, I said, "Nikos isn't actually on his deathbed…"

"Oh, I know that," Eleni said with a rueful smile. "Half the villagers have been on the telephone. They know how much the Dina means to me and knew I would want to be with her. She try to be brave but she is full with the worry for the Kostis' father."

"You do know that Kostis isn't here?"

"I know. He should be here; his parents need him at this time. Spiros says he thinks Kostis is off hunting the wild boar."

It would make a change from him being off hunting women. Instead of voicing my thought, I asked Eleni if Spiros had managed to contact Kostis.

"He try but the telephone he have not the reception in the high mountain," Eleni said.

"If it was possible to contact Kostis and he came home, would you stay, Eleni?"

"I would stay if Kostis would be the good husband and the good father to Nikoleta. She needs her *baba*." Eleni's voice reverberated with longing. Glancing at me shyly, Eleni continued with heartfelt emotion. "I love Kostis and I want my marriage to work but he act like the boy, not the man. The marry man should not to make the *kamaki* with the other women, he should be the responsible."

Dina's ears pricked up at the mention of her beloved son. Leaning forward, she placed a finger beneath Eleni's chin. Fixing her daughter-in-law with an unwavering look, she declared that Eleni was worth ten of Kostis. Blaming herself for Kostis' shortcomings as a useless husband, she admitted she had spoiled the boy and that his father had been too soft on him.

"*Alla otan ton afises, ton espase,*" Dina said, telling Eleni that when she left Kostis, it broke him. I struggled to understand all of Dina's speech as it was punctuated with sobs, but the gist of it seemed to be that she knew that Kostis would change if Eleni would only take him back and give him a second chance. The two women clung to one another, almost suffocating Nikoleta, trapped mid-embrace.

When Eleni went into the kitchen to grab a tea towel to mop up her tears, Dina slipped her arm around me. Winking at me, she whispered, "*Einai kalo pou o Nikos travmatistike an mou fernei tin Eleni.*"

I wasn't sure how Nikos would react if he heard his wife had just said that it was good that he was hurt if it brought Eleni back to her. I reflected that within this close-knit Greek family, Eleni was more than just Kostis' wife: in addition she was Dina's adored daughter-in-law, her passport to eventually hanging up the chip fryer and putting her feet up.

Plonking a plate of chips in front of Nikoleta, my mother demonstrated a depth of tact I would never guess she was capable of, whispering, "'Appen we should give them a bit of alone time, lad. Come on, I'll give you a hand scrubbing that mucky grill."

Chapter 22

No Fella's Punching Bag

T hat Nikos is a mucky bugger, look at all this grease caked on," Violet Burke grumbled.

"Considering the amount of meat I've enjoyed from that very grill, I'd rather not examine it too closely," I said, shuddering at the thought. Preferring to turn a blind eye to the thick layers of congealed grease, encrusted grime and ancient burnt bits, I tried to convince myself that it wasn't desperately unhygienic. Whilst still generally wary of dining in unknown restaurants where the staff may be lax in their hygiene habits, I had long relinquished my reservations about eating in the less than pristinely clean Meli taverna, won over by the superlative food and wonderful atmosphere on offer. At least all the meat that had been bunged on for grilling originated from Nikos' own organically reared stock which he assured me were germ free.

A worrying thought occurred to me. I hoped that Nikos didn't expect me to take over slaughtering and butchering the meat as part of my duties while I stood in for him. When Nikos delights in mocking me for being too squeamish and womanly to cook up one of my own chickens, I retain my manhood by fobbing him off with the excuse that my chickens are beloved pets. I could hardly claim the same close relationship to the animals he reared for food, but if the subject came up, I would refuse to engage in such a carve up. If Nikos pressed the matter, I would stand my ground and refuse to grill anything other than shop bought *souvlaki*.

Slapping the Marigolds on, my mother sprinkled a more than generous measure of powdered Vim over the filthy metal grill rack. Imagining Nikos' fury if the lamb ended up seasoned with Vim, I advised her to lay off the powder and tackle it with boiling water and elbow grease.

Without any prior warning, my mother hurled the cylindrical tub of Vim in the direction of a wilted basil plant.

"Drat. Missed it," she spat.

"Missed what?"

"There, behind that plant. I could have sworn it was that horrible cat of Cynthia's. Have a root round behind them plant pots, Victor. 'Appen you could grab hold of the ugly thing," she instructed.

"I prefer to keep my distance from the vile creature if it's all the same."

"Show some gumption, lad. We could have a right old laugh cooking it up instead of chicken."

Tempting though it was, I couldn't in all conscience serve up the scabby cat to the unsuspecting locals and risk a mass outbreak of food poisoning in the village. Anyway, it doesn't do to encourage my mother.

"Not only are there laws prohibiting that sort of thing, it would devastate Cynthia. She's only just been reunited with it," I protested.

"Lighten up, Son; I was just pulling your leg." Vi's words sounded remarkably unconvincing. "You wouldn't catch me eating foreign cat, it's likely ridden with bacteria. Now, pass me that old toothbrush, it will be handy for getting at the fiddly bits."

My stomach recoiled as I wondered whose mouth the used toothbrush had been intimate with. It was all very well to use such an implement to buff up the grouting between the floor tiles, but it was quite disgusting to think of it being used on something that would soon be in close proximity to the food I would be responsible for serving. I could only imagine the uproar if an ex-public health inspector was found guilty of starting an outbreak of diarrhoea.

Reflecting that once I got the hang of lighting the coals, the dry heat from the naked flames would serve as a steriliser killing off any active germ spores, I held my tongue. Violet Burke is not renowned for welcoming criticism of her cleaning methods. Besides, she had worries on her mind, fretting that she might be shown the taverna door now that Eleni had turned up. Dina's daughter-in-law posed no threat to Violet Burke in the thoroughness of scrubbing stakes, but being family she had the advantage of being exploitable without running up a wage bill.

"Even if Dina does replace you with Eleni, you've still landed those jobs cleaning for Moira and Sherry. If you weren't so bull-headed about learning a bit of Greek, you could probably pick up some cleaning jobs from the Athenians with second homes in the village."

"'Appen if they're rich enough to have two houses then they've got enough cash to pay for English lessons." My mother is always the pragmatist.

"Didn't Doreen mention something about

having you in weekly?"

"Aye, but I like it here. There's more going on...and Nikos and Dina never stand over me like the English do, faffing that I might have missed a bit. They have the good sense to trust that I'll just get on with the job. There's nowt worse than having someone mithering on behind me when I'm on my hands and knees with the scrubbing brush. Dina can chunter on all she likes, it makes not a blind bit of difference with me not understanding a word that she says. Pass me the bleach, lad. Hang on; will this lot explode if the fire hits the bleach?"

"Bleach isn't flammable but the heat from the coals might cause it to release a toxic vapour. It wouldn't do to risk gassing the customers. If I were you, I'd give the chlorine a miss and stick to hot soapy water."

Reluctantly relinquishing the bleach, Violet Burke spat on her cleaning cloth, saying, "I wish I could remember where I put my balaclava down, my head's fair icy. I had it when I bicycled over." Pushing her bucket to one side, she grabbed a chair, polishing off a splodge of splattered bird droppings before sinking her ample backside down.

"See, with the likes of that Sherry, she'll harp on and on. Just because she's paying me, the daft cow expects me to listen: likes the sound of her own voice way too much, that one. I told that Sherry straight, I'm here to clean, not to act as your unpaid psychic…"

"Don't you mean psychiatrist," I corrected.

"I know what I mean, lad. How am I supposed to know if she'll meet the right fella? That's what she's forever bleating on about. I mean, if you were a fella…"

"It may have escaped your notice but I am…"

"You know full well that I mean available like. You'd hardly want to put up with all that jolly-hockey-sticks guff…and as for them dentures of hers, I told her straight, they make her look right horsey. I mean if you were a fella, would you want them teeth of hers getting anywhere near your delicate bits?"

I considered it best to keep my own counsel about Sherry's attempt to seduce me. It didn't seem wise to give Violet Burke more ammunition.

"'Appen I'll have a word in the morning with that Tina in the shop about cleaning there, just in case Dina has to give me the boot. I remember you saying she was all right to work for when she took you on as a grocery boy."

"I was the temporary manager, not the grocery boy," I bridled. "But yes, Tina is fine to work for, it's her mother that you have to…"

"What lad?"

"Nothing." It seemed pointless to warn Violet

Burke about the wart- faced old hag, Despina, since I was sure my mother would be able to hold her own against the poisonous witch. In spite of not being a gambling man, I would put money on it. It would almost be worth enduring Despina's return to the shop to watch the battle of the harridans and see my mother take Despina down a peg or two.

"I was just hoping Barry turns up soon to show me how to light this grill."

"Aye, we could do with some warmth out here. It's that cold I can feel the chilblains on my feet mushrooming. I hope they don't mutate into something fungal."

"Never mind your feet. The customers will be arriving in short order expecting grilled fare. I don't suppose you know how to get this thing going."

"Aye, I had lots of practice barbecuing in my flat above the chippy, you daft apeth." A wink accompanied Violet Burke's sarcastic response.

"Probably best if I wait for Barry or Nikos…it looks a tad tricky."

"Aye, well think on, that Nikos will be putting a brave face on it when he drags his injured carcass down, even though he nigh on lost an arm and an eye today. He's of the same generation as me. You'll never hear us bellyaching on about our aches and pains; we just soldier on regardless…"

"Mother, I could write a book about your

endless complaints about your creaking joints and your swollen feet."

"You cheeky apeth; I ought to wash your mouth out with a good carbolic. Anyhow, you shouldn't mock, you might have inherited my feet. Just give it another twenty years and 'appen you'll get intimately acquainted with the same affliction."

"Let's hope I inherited my feet from that dodgy soap salesman, Vic."

"Well, he did have a limp. Anyhow, I was just saying, cut Nikos a bit of slack this evening…"

"If there's any slack to be cut, it's generally Nikos that needs to do the cutting."

"Aye, well. I was just warning you not to go all foot-in-mouth."

My mouth fell open at the irony of my mother's words. I seemed to spend my time doing little else than extricating Violet Burke's feet from her mouth, yet here she was warning me to go easy on my friend. If she wasn't careful, she was in danger of revealing her soft centre.

"Anyhow, lad, I don't know how we got started talking about slack but let's drop it. Slack isn't a word I like to hear…"

"What on earth have got against the word slack, Mother?"

"It brings back memories I'd rather not delve into, lad."

Clocking my raised eyebrows, Vi spat, "Since you insist on knowing all my business, Slack was one of my married names. And I'll have none of your lame jokes about slack in name, slack by nature: I've heard them all before."

"I'm not insisting on knowing your business, Mother, but I must confess to being naturally curious. Funnily enough, I was only thinking earlier that you've been very close lipped where husband number two is concerned. I don't believe you've ever brought him up."

"What's the point in regurgitating Reg Slack when he's ancient history, lad? Sometimes it's best not to go raking up old husbands. The things he yelled at me when he found out about you were summat I'll never forgive. Turned the air blue he did with his foul language and gave me a few right backhanders with his fists. I walked out on him there and then. I'm no fella's punching bag."

Shocked to the core that her brute of a husband had turned his fists on her, I reached over and squeezed and her hand.

"I promised myself that when he came round grovelling, I wouldn't take him back. Funny thing was, he never showed his face again; that pummelling was his final gift. Mind you, I was stuck being a Slack until I could divorce the bugger...nigh on twenty years I was saddled with Slack and then I went and traded it in for Blumenkrantz."

"It sounds as though you were well rid…"

"Aye, if I'd known what sort of ruffian he was under all his pretensions, I'd never have gone through with that wedding malarkey. Course with marrying in haste, I hadn't seen that side of him. If you take my advice, Victor, you'll never rush into marriage."

"It appears to have slipped your notice but I am already happily married."

"I'm hardly likely not to notice Marigold, she's not exactly invisible. Mind you, I'll say this for the pair of you, you've stuck at it and made it work. 'Appen you didn't marry in haste."

"It wasn't a long courtship…"

"Aye, Benjamin said you had to get wed because he was on the way."

"We would have got married anyway. Benjamin just speeded things along a little."

"Now me and Reg, or rather Reginald, he always insisted on going by Reginald even though it was a bit of a mouthful…we had what you'd call a whirlwind romance. Swept me off my feet he did; I was officially a Slack inside three weeks."

"When was this?" I asked.

"Back in the early 50s. He was a bit of a looker and always nicely turned out. He liked to say that after getting his hands on his Burton's demob suit, he promised himself he'd never go back to factory work and grimy collars, but make something of himself. Like I said, he was full of pretentions ever though he was as common as me. Course, I was a catch too, back then. There's not many a fella can resist a pair of shapely pins and a fulsome bosom hoisted up with a bullet bra."

"A bullet bra?"

"You must remember them pointy bosoms that were all the rage in the 50s, lad. I could have been taken for that Jayne Mansfield from the neck down when I had my Maidenform on."

I didn't bother questioning Violet Burke's inflated opinion that she'd been a catch back in the day: with four husbands and a string of admirers under her belt, she must have had some appeal.

"Anyway, with being respectably wed, I reckoned it was high time I had a go at repairing the family rift."

"They'd disowned you."

"Aye, but well more than a decade had passed and I had high hopes that they'd mellowed. I tell you, lad, I rue the day that I took Reg to the Blossom house. They only let us in right reluctantly because they didn't want to air their dirty laundry in front of the neighbours. Reg looked down his nose at them right off the bat, thought he was a cut above an outside lavvy and a tin bath. As for your grandparents, they'd gone full-on devout Methodist by then. Rather than healing the rift and letting bygones be bygones, straight off the bat they accused me of bringing shame on the Blossom name. They wasted no time dredging it all up, calling me a sinful harlot for getting myself pregnant out of wedlock."

"It wasn't all down to you. Vic played his part," I reminded her.

I reflected that it was no great loss that I'd never had the opportunity to meet the Blossoms: cold, unfeeling and unforgiving are unattractive traits. It was amazing that Violet Burke had turned out as she did after being raised by such a dour bunch of preachy temperance types.

"Reg couldn't drag me out of there fast enough when it all kicked off. Soon as we got on the street, he put on a right show for the neighbours, demanding to know why I hadn't come clean with him about my past before we wed. I told him we'd hooked up that fast there hadn't been time, we really knew nowt about each other."

"Three weeks isn't long," I agreed.

"I said to Reg, 'appen I had been keeping secrets but I never told any lies, I just omitted a few bits of my past. He demanded to know if it was true that I'd gone and got myself pregnant, so I fessed up about having you in the back of the chippy and all that bucket business. I remember him gawping at me as though I was a stranger, his eyes all cold and narrow. He said straight that he'd never have married me if he'd known I'd been intimate with another man...his language was fair blue when he shouted that he'd never have had owt to do with me if he'd known I was a trollop like his first wife. Turns out I wasn't the only one who'd been keeping secrets; he'd never breathed a word about being wed before. There he was getting all riled up because it came out he wasn't the first fella I'd hopped into bed with..."

Despite the shock I was experiencing hearing this, I couldn't help but notice that Violet Burke appeared to be downplaying her long list of bed partners.

"Talk about calling the kettle black. Reg wasn't exactly virginal himself, not that I wanted a wet behind the ears fella with no experience. When I told him he was nothing but a hypocrite, he went full-on ballistic, screaming at me that I had the morals of an alley cat and that I was no better than his first cheating wife. He grabbed me right rough like by the shoulders and shook me that hard my teeth fair rattled."

"There's never any excuse for a man to be violent towards a woman," I said.

"Well, I'd have steered well clear of his charms

if I'd known he was the sort of fella who reacted with his fists. He got all puce in the face, shouting about how he'd been wed before the war…then, when he got demobbed, he got home to find his wife up the duff by some Yank. That's when the bugger thumped me, right there with the Blossoms watching everything from behind their nets. I reckon he was lashing out at the both of us, the first wife and me. Them punches of his was hard enough to down two drunken navvies and I had a right shiner for weeks."

Appalled by the violence meted out to Violet Burke at the brutal hands of her second husband, I made a mental note to exclude Reginald Slack from my mother's eightieth birthday party if the wife-beating scoundrel hadn't already croaked it.

Tossing me the cleaning cloth she'd been using on the mucky grill, Vi said, "Here, lad. You'd best mop up them tears in your eyes. Nikos is coming and you don't want him winding you up about getting all soppy and womanly."

Chapter 23

Norman's Blasted Traffic Cones

Despite wearing his injuries with pride, Nikos looked as though the stuffing had been knocked out of him. There was a discernible hesitancy to his usually firm pace and it was clear from the pain in his one visible eye that his olive grove wounds were giving him gyp. His right arm was hoisted at an uncomfortable angle by the sling, fixed and immovable, while the elastic holding his eye patch in place left an angry red furrow etched across his forehead. Still, despite my expectations, he bore no resemblance to a pirate.

"Niko, are you sure that you're feeling well

enough to come down?" I asked.

"I hardly to leave the you to burn the place down," Nikos chortled, wincing as I knocked his injured arm with my clumsy hug. Brushing me off, Nikos stomped over to the grill. Eyeing it closely with his one visible eye, I could practically see the smoke coming out of his ears. His nostrils flared. "What you to do to the grill? He is clean."

Managing to make clean sound like a dirty word, Nikos appeared flabbergasted at the sight of the grill sparkling in the yellow rays cast by the bare light bulb dangling on a dodgy cable suspended from the grape vine. I imagine his fury would have been more vocal if he didn't appear lost for words.

It was a good thirty seconds before Nikos found his voice again. "Victor, how the meat to eat the flavour from the grill now?"

"Don't go blaming me, I had nothing to do with it," I protested, feeling a twinge of guilt for not shouldering the blame for my mother. It wasn't very manly of me to hide behind her skirts even if I hadn't had anything to do with scrubbing it clean.

"Like you to have the nothing to do with the fire when you to throw away the good oil from the fryer," Nikos accused.

"Leave it out, Niko. That was two years ago," I grumbled, thinking at least his memory was still as sharp as a tack.

"Let hope you set the nothing on fire this time…"

"Apart from the cooking charcoal," I quipped.

"You're a mucky bugger and no mistake, Nikos," my mother piped up, seemingly forgetting her assertions that Nikos should be treated with kid gloves. "If my Victor had been doing his health inspecting meddling, he'd have shut you down sharpish and no mistake. You should be ashamed of yourself letting that grill get so filthy. Have you never heard of hygiene standards?"

"I hear the little else since the Victor he move to Meli." Nikos' words were softened by a wink: at least I think it was a wink, it was a tad difficult to be sure in light of the eye patch.

"Well, I'm not standing around on these swollen feet listening to you carping because you don't appreciate a clean grill. I'm going indoors for a warm up. 'Appen that wife of yours knows what happened to my balaclava."

"Dina not cook the *baklava* today," Nikos replied.

"I should hope she didn't. It's not edible even if you do have some funny eating habits over here."

"You insult the Dina's *baklava*…"

Violet Burke slammed the door on Nikos' griping. Rather than getting bogged down attempting to describe the difference between the classic Greek pastry and my mother's bizarre choice of headgear, I asked Nikos how his injuries transpired.

"The Guzim. He use the *prioni* like the *spathi*, you understand?"

"He used the saw like the sword," I said, trying to imagine Guzim having an Errol Flynn moment in the olive groves. "So, what happened? Did he try to stab you through the eyeball?"

"No, he to let go of the branch and, how you to say, he rebound like the didgeridoo."

Nikos seemed so pleased with his analogy that I hesitated to burst his bubble by pointing out that he'd confused his didgeridoos with his boomerangs. Attempting to be subtle, I instead asked him if he could tell me the Greek words for the two items from down under. Noting from his reply that both words were the same in Greek and English, I made a mental note to add them to my ever expanding list of words that were the same in both languages. I could perhaps practice my conversational Greek by dropping an accented didgeridoo and boomerang into my next chat with any hitchhiking pensioners flagging me down with their walking sticks. Adam's advice to discover as many Greek words as possible that mirrored their English counterparts had proved invaluable since moving to Greece.

"You must to help the Dina with the olive

tomorrow…"

I interrupted to voice my objection before Nikos could complete his sentence. "I'm doing my bit by helping you out here." To prove my point, I showed willing by hoisting a sack of charcoal onto my shoulder and tipping the contents into the grill, nearly giving myself a hernia in the process. "I'll be worn out doing the evening shifts here."

"You have the stamina of the woman, Victor," Nikos teased. "You know the tomorrow many the old clap out pensioner to help the Dina."

I had to laugh at the way Nikos, a man in his late seventies, failed to include himself in the category of old and clapped out. Still, on reflection, I may be a veritable youth in comparison to Nikos and his cronies but they clearly had the edge on me when it came to stamina. In comparison to their hard lives of toiling in the fields and physical labour, I had been rather coddled in my illustrious career as a public health inspector.

"To be the serious, Victor, I appreciate you turning up to the help in the taverna. Dina cannot to be in the kitchen and to grill at the same time, and anyway, the cooking the meat is the work for the man. Without you to help, I must to padlock the restaurant."

"You're welcome, Niko. I wouldn't see you forced to close when I'm on hand to help. You can always rely on me, except when it comes to your olives."

"The Dina to think of you like the son…the better the son than the Kostis."

Bending over the grill, I attempted to fire some life into the charcoal, my face averted so that Nikos would not spot the tears pooling in my eyes.

"To think we to raise the boy who not be the here to help the *mama* in the time of need…we spoil him."

The side door leading into the taverna was flung open with such force that it nearly dented the stone wall.

"*Ela, Niko. Pos eisai, palioi apateones?*" I had no clue who the chap was who had just greeted Nikos, shouting, 'How are you, you old rogue?"

"*Christo. Pote epestrepses apo ti Thyellodi Poli?*" Nikos replied, asking Christos when he got back from the Windy City. If the chap had been off in Chicago, it was no wonder I'd never run into him before.

Short and stocky, Christos boasted boot-polished dyed hair and a luxuriant black moustache. Whilst clearly fitting into the pensioner category, he was much too hale and hearty to be lumped in with the clapped-out brigade.

Firing a dismissive look in my direction, the newcomer said to Nikos, "*Vlepo oti echete enan*

Alvano na kanei ti douleia tou skylou."

As I mentally translated his sentence to mean, 'I see that you've got an Albanian to do the dogs-body work,' Nikos used his remaining good arm to physically restrain me from attacking the conde-scending oaf with the cooking tongs.

"The Victor is not the Albanian, he is the English," Nikos said.

"English." Christos' demeanour instantly changed. Extending a hand in greeting, he crushed the bones in my barbecuing hand. "Things have changed for the better over here while I've been in the States. There's a cracking looker inside. I have the weakness for the redheads."

A saucy wink accompanied his American twanged words before he slipped into Greek vul-garities to describe a few choice things he wouldn't mind doing with the redhead. Biting back my retort that I'd rather he didn't speak about my mother like that, I realised that Violet Burke didn't exactly need me to act as her knight in shining armour and leap to her defence. She was more than capable of giving as good as she got. I expected she would have this bombastic Greek put in his place in short order.

After shooting the breeze a little more, Christos went back inside, quipping he didn't want his salad to get cold.

"The Christos he divorce now and come back to

the home in Meli. He live in the Chicago many the year," Nikos explained before warning me, "You want to lock up the Violet Burke. The Christos, he have always to play the ladies' man."

"It will make a change for my mother to be able to understand a Greek with a corny chat up line," I laughed, thinking of Panos' feeble attempts to sweet-talk my mother with sacks of spuds. Recently the local welly-wearing farmer had called by to ask if he could borrow my Greek to English pocket dictionary in order to brush up his courting skills. Thus far, he had mastered the odd polite greeting. Whenever I ran into him, he had started to greet me with a well-rehearsed and heavily accented, "Good Morning, Victor. You look very beautiful today."

As was only to be expected, the arriving villagers took it in turns to pop outside to check up on Nikos, word of his accident having spread through the village like wildfire. Litsa didn't linger, the black clad widow only staying long enough to give Nikos a rather sticky looking salve concocted from honey and a secret ingredient, to ease the bruising around his eye. Her brother Matthias followed hot on her heels; offering up a freshly peeled bulb of garlic, he swore it was the best remedy to bring the bruising out before telling me that he hoped 'my' Albanian's rabbit had recovered from being inseminated.

"I should to have eat the raw garlic to keep the safe distance from the Guzim. If I to smell as bad as the Matthias, the Guzim not to come near with the saw," Nikos joshed as Matthias made his way unsteadily back inside. I was impressed that Nikos was able to joke about his near fatal encounter, being too good-natured to bear a grudge against Guzim.

Giannis, the handsome bee man, was next out, eager to share with me the tale of 'my' Albanian's rabbit being deflowered. Tuning out as he rabbited on in indecipherable Greek, it struck me that I was as destined to end up chatting with the Greek villagers about Doruntina's first sexual encounter as I was to be stuck with talk of traffic cones and house prices from the expats. Before Giannis departed, we both agreed that 'my' Albanian was a touch too sensitive for his own good. I determined I really must make some effort to disabuse the villagers of the notion that Guzim was 'my' Albanian. The way they talked, anyone would think I had adopted the fellow.

It was a relief when Spiros rolled up, the local undertaker striking me as the type to be a tad more experienced in the pyromania department than me. My beyond pathetic attempts to light the barbecue had thus far resulted in nothing but a glimmer of an ember, extinguished the second the wind changed direction.

Carrying a platter of lamb chops that needed grilling for the ravenous hordes inside, the undertaker advised, "Niko, you should to take the weight off inside and leave the grilling to the Victor. Remember the doctor he to say you should to take to the bed."

"I cannot to trust to the Victor, he is the innocent. I must to stand over him to give the instruct," Nikos said.

"You the no use with one arm. Leave to the Victor. He not the innocent, he have the experience, he work here before," Spiros argued.

"He to do the woman work in the kitchen. The grill he is the man work and the Victor is good for the woman work. He too afraid to kill the chicken."

"It's just as well that it's lamb chops on the menu tonight then," I retorted, relieved that the pesky business of wringing necks and plucking feathers wasn't actually part of my job description.

Before Nikos could hurl any more disparaging slurs in the direction of my manhood, Barry joined us.

"Am I glad to see you," I greeted my brother-in-law. "I haven't got a clue how to get this dratted grill going. I've been at it for ages and Nikos barking orders at me hasn't helped."

"You should have said, I've been inside for the

last twenty minutes with Marigold," Barry said. Despite my wife's claim that she was coming along to keep me company, she hadn't so much as stuck her head outside to say hello. "Cyn and the baby came along too, and your mother stopped on for the company. Anastasia is that taken with Waffles that we might have to get her a puppy of her own."

"Blasted grill," I shouted, foiled in yet another attempt to light it. "The next time I go into town, I am going to buy Nikos a modern gas grill with simple controls. All this faffing around with charcoal and matches is practically stone-age."

"Get yourself inside, Victor. I'll sort out the grill and give you a shout when it's ready for you to start cooking on."

"Thanks, Barry."

"Don't get too settled. I should have it going in a jiffy."

My entrance was met with a stream of Greek expletives, the regulars engaging in their regular griping whenever the side door leading to the grill was opened to usher a blast of cold air in. Marigold and Cynthia were seated together. Violet Burke, having got her hands on her missing headgear, had balaclaved up. Bouncing Anastasia on her knee, she pulled the mask up and down over her eyes, playing peekaboo with the baby. For some inexplicable reason, the children in the extended Bucket family were all rather taken with my mother. My niece appeared to find it uproariously funny every time my mother fed Waffles a chip. It struck me that chips fried in oil would play havoc with Waffles' sensitive stomach. Since the flatulent dog would be spending the night with us, I rushed over to snatch the plate of chips away.

Joining my family, I was more than a tad taken aback to discover Marigold primping her Titian locks and giggling like a schoolgirl at something Christos had just said. The recent arrival from Chicago, having claimed a seat on the adjacent table, was blatantly chatting up my wife, Marigold unashamedly lapping it up. I reflected that when Christos had observed there was a redheaded looker inside who had tickled his fancy, I had naturally jumped to the assumption he was talking about Violet Burke since they seem much of an age. Since I'd had no idea Marigold had arrived, it was a reasonable conclusion to draw. Moreover Violet Burke had been banging on about what a catch she'd been back in the day. Never mind Nikos warning me to lock up my mother when Christos was in the vicinity, it appeared I needed to extricate my wife from his flattery.

"There you are, darling. Are you having fun playing at barbecuing?" Marigold trilled.

"I'm working, not playing."

"Hello, Son. I thought I'd stop on for a bite to eat seeing as the chops are being done on a clean grill for a change," my mother said.

"I'm so glad we offered to have Waffles overnight," Marigold gushed, stroking the dog's curly coat. I noticed that my wife had conveniently turned her offer to dog sit into a mutual decision, as if I'd had any say in the matter. "Look at Anastasia's face, she just adores him."

It was true; my niece was giddy with joy. Catching sight of the look of adoration on Christos' face as he gazed at my wife in admiration reminded me of the look on Waffles' face as he gulped down another chip. Determined not to stand by and be cuckolded by the cocky Chicagoan, I leaned over and hissed, "That redhead you think is a bit of all right is my wife."

"Oh, Victor, where are your manners? There's no need to be rude," Marigold said, basking in the attention of her new admirer.

"Not half as rude as some of the things he said he'd like to do to you," I snapped. Leaning in, I whispered in Marigold's blushing ear a few of the things Christos mentioned he fancied doing to her.

"That's disgusting." Marigold fired one of her withering looks at Christos before telling him in no uncertain terms, "I'll have you know that I am a happily married woman."

Christos responded by fondling his moustache and winking saucily at Marigold. Fortunately he was soon distracted by the arrival of an actual available woman as Sherry tripped into the taverna, wobbling in unsuitable heels.

"Oh, I thought Sherry was bringing the new man in her life." The disappointment in Marigold's tone was palpable.

Sherry's flapping ears picked up on Marigold's comment and she cooed, "My boyfriend will be here in a minute. He just stopped to pick some *horta* by the side of the road."

Marigold immediately perked up at this news, staring at the taverna door in anticipation of Sherry's new boyfriend revealing himself.

Everything went black; the taverna plunged into sudden darkness, prompting cries of, "What?" and "*Ti?*" to erupt in two languages.

"That will be Norman and his blasted flashing traffic cones," I groaned. "I just knew he'd go and overload the electrics."

Chapter 24

To Make the Dina Happy

As Dina and Eleni busied themselves depositing candles on the tables and patting themselves on the back for getting most of the chips fried before the power blew, Barry popped his head through the side door.

"The grill's ready for you now, Victor."

One of the advantages of cooking on an outdoor grill is that the lamb chops can continue to sizzle in spite of the unreliability of the electric supply. The taverna can remain open for business with atmospheric romantic lighting and heat radiating from the cast iron *somba*.

"Coming," I called back, annoyed that it was too dark for Christos to clock the additional warning look that I fired in his direction.

"Here, Victor. Do you want a lend of my balaclava? It'll keep your head cosy out there."

Pausing to decline my mother's kind offer, I noticed another customer entering the taverna. Through the candlelit gloom, I recognised him as Heinrich the German hippie. As he cautiously made his way across the room and joined Sherry, the final pieces of the mystery man jigsaw fell into place as I realised that the mullet sprouting from the back of Heinrich's receding hairline was well below shoulder length. I couldn't imagine Marigold would be too impressed to discover Sherry's new beau was an aging flower child with a scruffy mullet who was always on the cadge.

Heading back outside to the grill, I grabbed Barry by the arm, recalling that I hadn't run into Heinrich since the eco-conscious vegetarian hippie had blotted his virtuous woke credentials by purchasing a packet of sausages and a bottle of liquid Ajax when I'd been running the shop.

"Barry, you'll never guess who Sherry's secret bloke is. It's only that scruffy hippie, Heinrich."

"No," Barry gasped. "That free-loader who had that horrible Apollo table out of your downstairs storage?"

"The one and only," I confirmed.

"Well, that's a rum turn up for the books. Sherry was insufferable when we were doing up her place, too full of herself to mix with the help… and now she's seeing that creep with a compost toilet. Can you imagine her planting her posh bum down on his compost lav?"

"I'd really rather not," I snorted. "Remember when we carted that tacky Apollo table up to that derelict ruin he calls home?"

"And he had that shocking collection of heads heaped on the floor…he had us thinking he was a bit of a head-chopper until we sussed he collected tatty old figurines," Barry reminded me.

"I tell you Barry, I've come across some filthy kitchens in my time but Heinrich's stood out as particularly gross."

"I remember all that foul smelling green gunk he'd been cooking up…doesn't he scavenge for all his food?"

"Well, he claims he lives on nothing but vegetarian weeds but I caught him red-handed buying a packet of pork sausages."

"What a hypocrite…"

"According to my mother…"

"Who is not the most reliable source," Barry joshed.

"I think she might be onto something this time,

she does have an in as Sherry's cleaner. Anyway, my mother reckons that Sherry has been throwing her cash around on this new man in her life. I thought she was just coming out with her usual twaddle but it all makes sense now. Heinrich's always after something for nothing, I bet he's using Sherry because she's loaded."

"It makes sense. There's nothing attractive about her apart from her cash…"

"Victor, stop the gossiping like the woman and come to help the Spiros to cook the lamb," Nikos shouted over.

"I'll give you a hand too," Barry offered.

"Take over, Victor. I no the good at the cooking," Spiros implored. "And the Nikos can do the nothing with the arm in the swing."

"Well, it was good of you to muck in," I replied, grasping the cooking tongs and turning a couple of chops over.

Just then Marigold's head appeared at the side door and she called me over. "Victor, be a dear and take Waffles outside with you. That dreadful hippie that's just turned up is complaining that it's not hygienic having a dog inside while he's eating. Can you believe he's threatening to report its presence to the authorities as a hygiene violation?"

"I'm surprised that long haired lout has even heard of hygiene," I scoffed. Taking Waffles' lead, I led the dog over to the others, delighted when it immediately responded to my command to 'sit' by actually planting its rear end on the ground, staring up at me doe–eyed.

"We have been to talking about the Kostis," Spiros confided. "The Nikos he want us to go up the mountain to find the son and to make him come home."

"What mountain?" I asked.

"The Kostis go to the hill to hunt. When he to go for the days at the time he stay in an old shepherd hut," Spiros explained. "I think we must to go look for the him."

Exchanging a knowing look with Barry, I surmised he had come to the same conclusion that we were both about to be dragged up the mountain in search of Nikos' errant son.

Adopting a wheedling tone, Nikos unleashed the full force of his persuasive spiel on us. "The Kostis, he go because the Eleni leave him and too late he realise he love the wife. Now the Eleni is here but the Kostis he not to know it…he could to miss the chance to fix the marry."

"The *kinito tilefono* he have no the signal in the hill," Spiros added, referencing Kostis' mobile.

"If you can to find him and make him to come home to repair the marry, the Eleni will stay," Nikos continued. "If the Eleni and the Nikoleta to stay, the Dina will be the happy to burst. Nothing will to bring me so big the pleasure as seeing the Dina joy to have the Eleni and the granddaughter to live with her again."

I must confess to finding Nikos' words intensely moving, his love for his wife evident in his heartfelt pleas, his desperation to make Dina happy by bringing the family together. Moreover, Nikos' words made me feel ashamed at the way I had so casually dismissed Marigold's desire for us to renew our wedding vows. Although I personally didn't see the point of going through the whole rigmarole, Marigold had repeatedly told me how happy it would make her: in return I had done nothing but continually douse her dreams with buckets of cold water. Determined to follow Nikos' example and be a better husband by putting Marigold's feelings first, I was about to suggest to Barry that we should most definitely go with Spiros and search for Kostis, when Barry pre-empted me.

"You know, Victor, I think the two of us should go with Spiros to search for Kostis. I don't mind admitting that Nikos' words have moved me. Being a new father myself, I know how important it is for Eleni and Kostis to reunite and for Kostis to develop a bond with Nikoleta. Just think how happy we will make Dina if we bring her son home with us and his marriage is saved."

"So, we must to go to the hill." Spiros' tone was emphatic.

"Count me in," I assured him.

"We go now..." Spiros urged.

"Finish the cook first. We have the hungry customer wait inside," Nikos reminded us.

"How are we going to get up there?" I asked. "I've just had the Punto cleaned and don't fancy risking its suspension on off-road terrain. Shall we take your builder's van, Barry?"

"It might not make it. Athena rear-ended it earlier," Barry reminded me.

"Well, Cynthia's old banger then."

"I pranged that when I rear-ended Panos' tractor."

"We take the hearse," Spiros volunteered.

"Victor, the dog!" Nikos cried.

To my horror, I saw that whilst we had been chatting, Waffles had knocked all the lamb chops from the grill to the filthy ground. The dog was tucking into them with such relish that one would think it hadn't been fed for a week.

"Your dog, Victor," Nikos shouted again.

"It's nothing to do with me. Blame Marigold," I said, happy to pass the can.

Our escape to the hills looked more inviting by the minute. With the amount of half-cooked lamb Waffles was scoffing, the goldendoodle would likely keep Marigold up all night, its sensitive stomach reacting to an overload of fatty meat. At least my absence would spare me from Marigold nagging me to take it outside each time its bowels were in danger of exploding.

"First the no electric, now the no lamb chop," Nikos groaned.

"I bring the hearse," Spiros said.

"This had better not turn into a wild goose chase," I muttered.

Chapter 25

Envious of Guzim's Shed

The sensation of something crawling up my leg woke me from a fitful slumber, the stony ground beneath my body digging into my bones uncomfortably through my cold, damp clothes. Through the doorless opening that offered the only window onto the world from our dank and gloomy environ, I could just discern dawn breaking, the morning twilight offering blessed relief from the interminable night.

It felt strange waking up without Marigold by my side. I imagined that she must have been out of her mind with worry when I failed to return home the previous night. I wondered if she took solace in having Waffles for company or if constantly attending to its bathroom needs had driven her to distraction. Considering the amount of chips and chops the dog had devoured, I supposed it must be more flatulent than ever.

The crawling sensation returned. Shaking my leg, an enormous black spider fell from inside my trouser leg, scuttling away towards the coffin. Its crab-like movement terrified me with the thought that the arachnid may have been a tarantula. It was still too dark to examine my flesh for any tell-tale fang marks.

I was amazed that I had managed to sleep at all with the chilly night air seeping into my bones and the din of Barry snoring beside me on the rough-hewn dirt floor. Spiros was still sleeping too: stretched out stiffly in the coffin, he put me in mind of a comfortable corpse. Naturally, Spiros had generously suggested that we take turns to rest in the padded casket. Considering it a tad morbid to say the least, I had declined the offer to take my turn at grabbing forty winks in the coffin we had dragged up the hill from the fuelless hearse.

I recalled our self-congratulatory mood the previous night when the three of us came within spitting distance of Kostis' hunting hideaway, patting ourselves on the back for being in hair's breadth of accomplishing our mission. Having successfully negotiated the rugged mountain terrain in the pitch dark, all we had to do was drag Kostis out of his shelter, bung him in the hearse, and return him to the bosom of his family. To our horror, just as we were feeling prematurely smug, the hearse ran out of petrol, leaving us stranded and forced to scramble and grope our way up the last quarter-kilometre on foot.

"It is not the problem," Spiros had assured us when we complained only a numbskull would neglect to top up the tank before starting out. "We wake the Kostis and send him on the *motosykleta* to bring back the petrol."

The fatal flaw in Spiros' plan became clear when there was no sign of Kostis' motorbike outside the run-down old shepherd's hut he used as his base. Clapping eyes on the ruined structure, my heart sank, knowing that if Kostis wasn't inside, we would be stuck there for the duration.

From the outside, the hut was a round stone windowless structure with a semi-caved in roof, featuring a low aperture that served as an entrance. Venturing inside, I was shocked by the state of humble decrepitude, the building cold and barren, lacking all basic amenities and any imagined home comforts. The only evidence that Kostis had been kipping down there was a filthy vermin-ridden blanket that looked capable of walking out under its own steam, a couple of discarded beer cans, a solitary loo roll and a pile of well-trodden cigarette butts. Kostis wasn't there, scuppering our plan to send him off to buy petrol. We were left with no other choice but to overnight there. Even if it hadn't been too dangerous to life and limb to attempt a descent of the steep hill in the darkness, the distinctive cry of wolves nearby frightened us into staying put.

"Victor, he is not the wolf, he is how you say, the jackass," Spiros had attempted to reassure me.

"I'm not going out there with jackals roaming at large," I said firmly.

Cowed by the thought of wild vicious dogs wandering loose, Barry flatly refused to set foot outside before daylight in jackal ridden territory. I felt less of a sissy knowing I wasn't the only coward amongst us.

"At least we don't have to worry about nettle rash on our nethers," Barry had quipped, grabbing the loo roll and heading off to find a discreet spot outside close to the exit.

As I'd looked around the dingy, rank smelling room, I couldn't help but compare it to Guzim's stone shed at the bottom of my garden. Considering the disparaging abuse I had heaped on his humble home by referring to it as a slum, Guzim would be having the last laugh if he could see the state of the place I was forced to bed down in. In comparison to the ruined shepherd's hut, the Albanian shed dweller's place was a veritable palace. How I envied Guzim at that moment; blissfully cuddled up with the warm and furry Doruntina in the pink palace of love.

When Barry sheepishly returned, he took one sniff of the foul blanket and hurled it outside, grumbling that if he'd only known what we were in for he would have accepted Violet Burke's offer to lend him her balaclava: it could have served as a makeshift pillow.

"What are we going to do?" he asked. Clearly Barry was out of his comfort zone being away from the village, not to mention his old complaint of travel sickness had reared its nauseous head on the journey.

"We have no the choice but to wait for the light and then to go with the feet. The good thing is we will not to starve," Spiros said, turning out his pockets to reveal a couple of filthy lamb chops covered in muck that he must have retrieved earlier. The beam from my torch highlighted the visible chew marks; it wouldn't surprise me to discover Spiros had wrenched the meat from the jaw of the goldendoodle.

"Don't even think of eating them, Spiro," I warned. "The dog trod on them and they're likely riddled with bacteria from the dirty ground outside the taverna."

"They will be the fine," Spiros argued, his stomach rumbling loudly. "They are only the little raw inside."

"Spiro, just listen to Victor for once. If there's one thing he's an authority on, it's germs. Think on, we'd have a right job carrying you back to civilisation if you come down with a nasty dose of food poisoning," Barry reasoned. "Besides, there's only a bit of that toilet roll left if you get the trots."

Reluctantly, Spiros tossed the chops outside, rashly disregarding any thought that the meat might entice flesh hungry jackals.

Groping through his pockets, Spiros triumphantly announced, "*Koita*, I have the *halva*." There was method in his munificence of sharing the local confectionary between us, Spiros blatantly using it as a bribe so we would help him drag the coffin up from the hearse to serve as a bed.

As daylight broke, I wished I'd given the *halva* a miss. The sweet nougaty residue still stuck in my teeth made me think longingly of the toothbrush my mother had used to scrub Nikos' grill. Looking at my two companions, I decided against waking them. They may as well enjoy another hour before waking to our dismal reality.

Dragging myself off the floor, I stooped my way through the low entrance, stepping outside onto the hillside. Gazing into the distance, I found myself entranced by the spectacular green vista shrouded in hazy light, wild sage bushes carpeting the rolling hillside amid fir and pine trees. Clusters of wild flowers, perhaps confused spring had arrived early, added a splash of colour to the rich tapestry. Greedily drinking in the clean sweet air redolent with wild herbs kissed by morning dew, I felt my spirits lift.

Our mission may have been nothing more than a fool's errand since we had failed in our plan to return Kostis to the bosom of his family, not to mention our sacrifice in slumming it overnight in that hovel, but our noble efforts would be appreciated. Looking into the distance, I found it impossible to gauge how far we had travelled in the dark, but I was up to the challenge of making it home to Meli on foot.

"You to hear that, Victor?"

Spiros' question startled me. I hadn't heard him climb out of his coffin and join me outside.

"No. What did you hear?"

"Listen."

My heart leapt at the distinctive sound of a motorbike approaching the hut. Kostis roared into view, helmetless with a shotgun slung over one shoulder, a brace of birds over the other. *Who was I kidding*? I thought to myself: what romanticised claptrap had I been thinking imagining traipsing kilometres back to Meli would be some kind of idyllic stroll in the park without so much as a coffee to sustain me.

Ten minutes later, Kostis clued up on Eleni's return and ready to make a go of his marriage, roared off on the motorbike to the nearest petrol station. Kostis gave Spiros the thumbs up as the undertaker yelled after him, "*Kosti, min xechasete na ferete treis kafedes kai merikes tyropitas*."

Barry, woken by the noise, popped up beside me just in time to see the motorbike soaring away. Rubbing his bleary eyes, he asked, "What was Spiros shouting about?"

"He was just reminding Kostis not to forget to bring three takeaway coffees and some cheese pies," I said.

"Cheese pies. I couldn't half murder a Fray Bentos right now."

A Note from Victor

I hope you enjoyed this latest Volume in the
Bucket saga.

All reviews gratefully received, even a word or
two is most welcome.

Please feel free to drop me a line if you would like
information on the release date of future volumes
in the Bucket to Greece series at
vdbucket@gmail.com
or via Vic Bucket on Facebook.

I am always delighted to hear from happy readers.

Printed in Great Britain
by Amazon

39417050R00195